Street Dreams for God's Child

Jeffrey Barlatier

KB&G Publishers

Street Dreams for God's Child

Published by Kingdom Book and Gift LLP
P.O. Box 291975
Columbia, SC 29229
803-736-2472

ISBN 978-06151-6458-8
Library of Congress
Printed in the United States of America

Contents

Acknowledgements   04

Part I-   *It all started...*

Chapter One: Genesis   07

Chapter Two: Married Life   11

Part II-   *Just steady tripping...*

Chapter Three: Reminisce   15

Chapter Four: Virginia, here we come!   21

Chapter Five: Back to Egypt   25

Part III-   *Things started to change...*

Chapter Six: Moving on up, to the Eastside   31

Chapter Seven: New Jersey Drive   37

Chapter Eight: Long Island Iced Tea   42

Part IV-   *Things fall apart...*

Chapter Nine: My Hobby, My Girlfriend and I   51

Chapter Ten: Up North   59

Chapter Eleven: D   61

Part V-   *Steady falling...*

Chapter Twelve: Switch   66

Chapter Thirteen: Thug Life   75

Chapter Fourteen: A New Fling   84

Part VI-   *One more chance...*

Chapter Fifteen: The Job   90

Chapter Sixteen: I'm Home   104

Acknowledgements

First and foremost, I would like to thank Jesus Christ who is the head of my life for inspiring me to pen these words to this paper. I would like to dedicate this book to my grandmother, Melina Civil. She is not alive to see this book but the words that she spoke into my life will always be remembered. I would like to thank my loving wife who is my backbone. You are the second best thing to come into my life aside from Jesus. Every morning I see you with that ring on your finger, you remind me that prayer works. I would like to thank my mother and father, my brother, John, Gilberte, Emmanuel, Mindy, Vanessa, Stephanie and Ruth. I do not know where I would be if it were not for them and if it were not for my loving Pastor and Overseer, Hezekiah Walker. Overseer Walker and the Love Fellowship Tabernacle are my second family and I am glad that God has placed them in my life. Where would I be without my boy, Kevin? God only knows. Thank you for believing in me even when others thought you were crazy for doing so. You saw things in me that I didn't even see in myself. Mom, thank you for coming to see me when I was at my lowest. You are by far the greatest mother in the world. John, thank you for protecting me and being the best brother any one could ask for. Much love goes out to brother Jason, Estee, Eric, Poka, Has, Cola, Troy, Ant, Ronald Bryant, Gerald, Mark, Denise, Desmond, Pastor Hugh, Pastor Chad Hinson and Elder Neil Harris. Thank you Silas and Lorenz for being the best children a father could ask for. Thank you to all those who always believed in me and told me what I would be even when I wasn't who I am now. Special thanks to all of the haters that never thought I would be nothing. To the ones that told me I dance too much, you are my greatest motivation and at the same time my greatest footstool.

Part I

It all started ...

Chapter One

Genesis

I remember that small bed my brother and I used to share, in that 2-bedroom apartment in East Flatbush. Anytime either one of us would move, the bed would make a loud noise. I hated that bed. 21 Parkside Avenue was the address, apartment 2B. We were living there for as long as I could remember. The paint on the walls was chipping and the entire apartment was infested with roaches. My father came to this country when he was in his early twenties. My father was originally from Haiti. Years ago, my aunt told me that my father used to hang out in the streets of Port au Prince, day in, and day out. Him and his friends would go from club to club and from party to party starting as much trouble as they could. My father was the smallest in the group but he had the most mouth. One day while he was on his way to a local party, my father came across a man that was preaching the Gospel of Jesus Christ in front of an abandoned building. The building was an old shabby church that was burned down some years ago by the local voodoo priest. No one in my family knows exactly what the man said to my father, but that night he ran home with tears in his eyes and told his mother that he was saved from his sins. After his encounter with the preacher, he was never the same. My father never told anyone what the preacher said to him, but whatever he said changed him for the rest of his life. My father became a missionary and began going into areas in Haiti that were predominantly populated by zombies. Zombies are dead people that are brought back to life through means of Vodoun or necromancy. After a few months he was led of the   Lord to go and preach the good news of Jesus in the United States. My father and his sister saved up enough money to send one of them to the United States. Their plan was to send my father first, and he would get a job and save up enough money so he could send for his sister and mother. And that he did.

My father arrived in Brooklyn in 1978. At the time, afros and bell-bottom pants were the latest trends. There was an extreme black consciousness movement going on. The Black Panther Party was on the rise, and so was hip-hop. He began looking for a job and preaching the Gospel of Jesus on trains, buses and everywhere else the opportunity arose. Half the population in Brooklyn didn't understand what he was saying because he was preaching in Creole (Haitian dialect), but a large amount of the people in Brooklyn did. By this time, many immigrants were coming into the United States and most of them would find themselves flocking to the familiar enclaves of Brooklyn. Brooklyn was slowly becoming the unofficial capital for immigrants coming in from the Caribbean. It was the "Mecca" of "platanos and fried fish," and every corner had either a deli that served Caribbean food or a group of men talking in the many dialects that the Caribbean is known for.

One day while my father was on the D train preaching about God, a man overheard him and walked up to him. It turned out that the man was a Pastor and he just opened up the first Haitian church in Brooklyn. He invited my father to come and preach at his church. My father accepted the offer and preached his first sermon at the little Haitian church in East New York. The Pastor asked my father to stay and become one of the ministers at the church. At the time the church only had two other ministers and my father could be a great help to his ministry. The church had very humble beginnings with only 15-20 members, but they were extremely faithful. They would have tarrying service all night. The praying they did in that little church was unheard of and was something the Apostles would have been proud of. They would pray for hours. They stood on the street corners and witnessed to people about the goodness of Jesus Christ. Many of the Haitians that heard them proclaiming the good news of Jesus also became faithful members. My father preached every other Sunday and the church began to blossom.

The Pastor of the church was married with seven children, five girls and two boys. My father began to fall in love with the Pastor's youngest daughter. She was a very pretty girl. She was five feet, five inches with light brown eyes and all the men in the church were attracted to her, and even some women. Some even said that she was the prettiest girl in the church. At the time my father was 23, and she was only 15. In the Haitian culture an age differences like this was normal, so age wasn't the issue to them. The problem was that Haitian parents didn't believe in dating. When her parents found out they were in love with each other, they quickly pressed the issue of marriage. Her mother was the most adamant about it. She told my father that if he didn't marry her they could not date. My father was a strong believer in getting married but he couldn't marry her at the time because he didn't have enough finances to pay for a wedding and he still had to save money to send for his sister and mother back in Haiti. So my father and the pastor's daughter stopped dating for the time being. But Every Sunday when he saw her, his heart would long for her, as hers did for him. They were in love.

My father continued to preach at the church every other Sunday, and the church continued to grow. By this time the church had around 500 members. Many of the women had their eyes on my father, especially when they found out that he was no longer dating the Pastor's daughter. He was handsome, single and could preach. As the church began to get larger the Pastor's wife continued to press the issue of my father marrying her daughter. My father told her he still had intentions on marrying her but he was still in the process of saving up enough money for the wedding. The Pastor's wife told him that she would pay for the wedding and that he could pay them back later. My father accepted the offer and two weeks later the wedding was held at the church.

Chapter Two

Married life

Married life was a little difficult for both of my parents. My father was from a traditional background, where the man worked and the woman stayed at home to cook, clean and take care of the children. The pastor's daughter was also from the same traditional background, but she didn't have plans on living the traditional life. My mother had six siblings and her father was the Pastor of the first Pentecostal Church in Brooklyn. Now if anyone knows anything about Pentecostal churches, they know that they are very strict. They strictly adhere to the teachings of the Bible. She wasn't allowed to do anything, and I mean this literally. She couldn't wear makeup, jeans, lipstick, red nail polish, go to the movies and had to wear a long skirt every day of the week. When she married my father she saw it as a way of escape. It was a way to break out of the old tradition and Haitian customs her parents had forced upon her. It was a new life.

Three months into the marriage, still 16 at the time, the pastor's daughter was pregnant by my father. By then my father had saved up enough money for his sister and mother to come to America. When his mother arrived she stayed with him and his new wife and his sister stayed with one of her cousins who had come to the United States some years prior. My father's mother helped out around the house. She cooked, cleaned and ironed all of my father's clothes. She always treated my father like he was still a little boy. He was after all her only son. I learned later on in life that my father never had a relationship with his father and that his mother always tried to make up the difference with the love and attention that she showed him.

They decided to call the baby John. The entire family believed that all children should have Biblical names, so my father chose the name John because he loved John the Baptist. Four months later my mother was pregnant again with another boy, me! My mother was only 17, married to a preacher with two kids and still in high school. My father was ready to have a family and my mother was ready to finally live her life the way she wanted to live it, even though things weren't going according to plan. My parents never really had the opportunity to date and get to know each other. So there were a lot of things that were expected in the marriage that was not happening. Haitian/Christian parents did not believe in dating. When a man was interested in a woman that he found attractive, he would meet with the girl and her parents to have a sit down and discuss the options. The parents were very involved in the screening process. My father assumed that since my mother was the daughter of the Pastor, and came from a traditional Haitian background, that my mother would follow in the Haitian traditions. Women in Haitian culture are very submissive and are taught from their youth how to treat a man. He thought that she was going to stand side-by-side with him as he proclaimed the Gospel of Jesus Christ. The Pastor's wife gave my father that impression when she continually told my father that he should marry her daughter. But her impression and his expectations were two frogs from different ponds.

Part II

Just steady tripping...

Chapter Three

Reminisce

I don't remember too much about my childhood, I just remember different scattered scenes of my early childhood. But it's funny the things I do remember. I remember never seeing my parents kiss, hug or show any type of emotion or affection towards each other. I loved watching movies but I wondered in my little adolescent mind, why they weren't like the people in the movies that would kiss and say "I love you" to each other. The closest I have ever seen them come to being intimate, was when my mother would put on a sweet voice and then ask my father for money. He would reply that he didn't have any and she would continue to ask until they would begin to argue and my father would walk out. He would leave and we would never know where he went.

Sometimes he would stay, but if he did, my mom would nag him for money until he either gave it to her or just got up and left.

I remember my father taking me and my brother fishing. My father loved fishing, but we hated it. We found nothing more un-exciting than having a million questions about life on the tips of our tongues, being in an environment that we could pose those questions, and not asking them, out of fear of course. We sat silently, watching my father smile as he looked out into the sunset as he waited for the catch of the day. Maybe it was a fear of him giving us a beating. I'm not really sure what we were afraid of, but we were always afraid. Don't get me wrong we looked up to him, but we never really had a relationship with him. We rarely spoke. I remember when we would go to church all the kids would run up to him and hug him. He would smile and hug them back. He seemed to come to life when he hugged the other children. The other children would look at us, and the looks in their eyes were looks of kids wishing they were the children of my father. He was well known throughout the Haitian community. When he walked into a room he commanded the attention of everyone, without uttering a single word. We learned at an early age that my father was well respected and people showed us extra love, just because of him. When we were with him in public we felt important. But when we were with him in private we had the same look that the children that loved my father had in their eyes. The look wishing they were his children. He never really hugged us like that. I remember always getting into fights at school, or should I say always getting jumped by a gang of school kids. I remember my brother would find out who they were and go and fight each and every one of them. He would always win. I remember my father playing soccer around the corner from our house and my brother and I watching him play, wishing we could someday be as good as him.

Jeffrey Barlatier

I always wanted to be like my father. Everything about him was amazing. He had wavy hair. He was very flamboyant with his clothes, and even though he didn't have a whole lot of money, he looked like a million bucks wherever he went. There was a certain air about him. I would always rush behind him every time he had to go to church, and that was all the time. We were always in church. I would see my father putting on his nice suit, with the shirt matching the tie and the tie matching the shoes. He would have the best cologne on. You could smell it from a mile away. I would always say to myself that I wanted to be just like him when I grew up. I know my brother said the same thing, even though he didn't talk a lot. My brother was what some might consider shy but those who knew him knew he was just quiet.

One time when my father was getting dressed for church and I wanted to go so bad. "Popi, can I go with you to church pleasssssssse?"(Popi was a Nickname we gave my father), I asked. He was quiet for a few seconds and then he said "hurry up". I ran to my mother and asked her where my church clothes were. "In your closet" she said with her eyes glued to the television. I ran as fast as possible and started putting on my clothes. My brother asked me where I was going and I told him "with Popi to church". He quickly started putting on his clothes too. Then all of a sudden we heard the door slam. We went into the room to ask my mom who came in the house, and she said "no one, it was your father leaving". We ran to the window hoping it wasn't true, but to our surprise it was. My father drove off and left us. That was the first time he ever did that, but it was definitely not the last. I will never forget that day. I always wondered why he did that. Most kids hated going to church but we loved it. We associated church with my father. We didn't listen to any of the sermons or anything but we loved it because we got a chance to be with our father, even if he didn't say much to us. As long as we were there with him we

17

were happy. It was the only time we really spent time with him, even though we weren't spending time with him.

By the time I were seven years old, the church was at its prime. On any given Sunday there would be close to 7,000 people at service. It just kept growing and growing. During the eighties and nineties, a lot of Haitian immigrants were coming to the United States, and the first place any Haitian would go would either be Miami or Brooklyn. When they came to Brooklyn they would eventually come to my grandfather's church. It was the Mega, Haitian church of the eighties. I stayed in church a lot as a kid. We practically lived there. My mom didn't go with us though. I figured that she probably went to church so much as a kid that she needed some time off. But she never went. Well, let me not say never. She came once. I still have pictures of that day.

Living in a house with my parents was like living in L.A. during the riots. My parents were always arguing. Every second there was an argument. My mother would go out to clubs and parties and my father would yell at her for going. He would tell her that she's a Christian and that she shouldn't be going to clubs and parties, but she wouldn't listen, she was having fun. She was living the life that she always wanted but her parents kept secluded from her. There were plenty of times my mother would take us to one of her female friend's houses and leave us there all night. She would do this so my father could think that she stayed at her friend's house all night, while she danced the night away. She would go to the clubs with her new outfit, hair done, nails done, mink coat on her back and diamond rings on every finger. Then she'd come stumbling in the door around five in the morning. We would be lying there pretending that we were sleeping and she'd come over to us and tell us how much she loved us. I think the reason that we pretended to be asleep was because we didn't want to have to say it back, at least not while she was drunk.

Between 8 and 10 years of age my life took on a strange shift. I say strange because a lot of the things that happened in those years didn't make sense to me. My mother had a best friend named Anna. Now I always had a crush on Anna.   Anna was 5'2, redbone complexion and weighed about 125lbs. I thought she was the prettiest woman on the planet.   So whenever my mother would go over there I would get happy because my brother and I were going too. Anna had an older brother named Kyle. I thought Kyle was the coolest guy in the world. He was light-skinned, bald-headed, 5"11 and he was muscular. He also walked pigeon-toed.   I used to always tell myself that when I grew up I would look like Kyle, and since I was already pigeon toed I figured being like him was a guarantee.

One day my mother took my brother and me to Anna's house. Anna wasn't home but Kyle was. My mother told my brother and me to wait downstairs. We went downstairs and waited. Now we had to be waiting downstairs in front of the project building for at least 5 minutes but when you're that age it feels like 5 hours. I told my brother that I was going back upstairs because I had to use the bathroom. So he said, "fine" and stayed down stairs and waited in the lobby. I never wondered what my mother was doing. I just wondered why it was taking her so long, especially since Anna wasn't there. She lived on the 3rd floor and the elevator was taking too long. I had to go really bad so I took the steps. When I got in front of Anna's apartment door, there they were. I couldn't believe my eyes.   My mother and Kyle were tongue kissing with the door wide open! I was only standing there for a quick second and I guess Kyle saw me and turned around real fast and started walking towards the back room. My mother looked at me grabbed me by my jacket and said "Didn't I tell you to wait downstairs!" I had to use the bathroom" I replied. We got into the elevator and went home. I never understood why I saw my mother kiss another man but I never saw her kiss my father.

A few months after that incident, my mother decided to leave my father. My mother never told us why she was leaving or even why she was taking us with her. She left my father and brought my brother and I for the ride. We didn't understand why we couldn't stay with our father. We begged our mother to let us stay with our father but all of our petitions landed on deaf ears. She took us to her sister's house in Virginia. Most of her siblings had gotten married and made the move down to Virginia and so she decided to follow suit. Maybe she could live the life she had so earnestly tried to acquire in New York, down in Virginia. Little did she know that, wherever you go, there you are.

My brother and I were both sad and happy at the same time. We were sad that we were leaving our father but we were happy we were going to live with my mother's sister, Aunt Rachel. Everyone loved Aunt Rachel. She was nice and she would always listen to us. She never yelled and when either one of my cousins or us had issues with our parents we would always run to Rachel. She was the one that put everything into perspective. She was the best, and now we were on our way to live with her.

Chapter Four

Virginia, here we come!

The ride to Virginia wasn't that bad. We hopped on the greyhound bus from Manhattan and arrived there in 5 hours. As soon as we saw Rachel at the gate waiting for us we ran to her and hugged her. It felt good hugging Rachel. She was full of love. She never had kids of her own but she had 6 nieces and nephews at the time to keep her busy and that we did. She took us to her condo that she had in Springfield, Virginia. I had never been in a condo before, and you know what the greatest thing about it was? She had no roaches! Can you believe that? Not a single one. The condo was immaculate. This was the kind of place people dreamed about. John and I shared a room while Rachel and my mom shared hers. We were starting a brand new life, and it felt good. Maybe this time it would work.

Another one of my aunts only lived about 15 minutes away from Rachel, her name was Mary. She was my mother's oldest sister. She had a family and lots of money. I liked Mary. She had two boys named Nate and JR. They were my cousins. Nate was the oldest out of all of us and JR was the youngest. Nate was tall for his age and he was a high school basketball superstar. He would tend to get into a little trouble here and there but Aunt Mary would put him in his place even before his dad would. Mary was married to Dan. Dan was tall and he used to be a high school basketball star too. Mary liked sports too so everything was perfect.

JR played soccer, basketball and baseball and he would always get trophies in each sport he played. He was an all-around athlete. I liked Dan because he was what a typical dad was, both in the way he acted and looked. He would always hug Nate and JR and tell them that he loved them. I only saw stuff like that on TV but never in real life, until I saw them. I wanted to be a part of their family. My brother did also. We were always there, and we never wanted to leave. We were there so much that Mary started giving us weekly chores and if we cleaned up the whole week we would get an allowance. Before I met them, I never knew what an allowance was. This was all new to me. Their house was big so there was always something to clean. Dan worked for a mattress company and he was making a pretty good salary there. But Mary was making crazy money. She was a nurse and she would work so much overtime that it should have been illegal. They had a Benz, a Lexus and a beautiful town home in Burke, Virginia. Nate and JR always had on the freshest clothes and even their haircuts were fresh. Nate had the Gumby fade and JR had the NAS low cut fade. They were living the life. I think they knew that my mother didn't really have any money like that, so Mary would always buy us stuff. She bought us food, clothes and even paid for me to play in the basketball league. They were big on sports. I loved being with them because they made us feel like part of the family.

My mother was supposed to be looking for jobs out there but since we moved down there, 3 months passed and she still hadn't found a job. Her dream of living the life she wanted was diminishing every day. One day I heard her on the phone with my father arguing over money and the next day she told us that our father was coming to see us. We were ecstatic. You would have thought someone told us we were winning a million dollars. We got dressed and waited. When my father finally arrived he gave us that smile that he gave everyone to show that he was happy. He had a little gap in between his teeth so it always showed when he smiled. We ran to him but we didn't hug him because...well we just never hugged him before. We shook his hand and said, "Hi, Popi!" That's how we always greeted our father, with a handshake. I would have loved to hug him the same way Rachel hugged us, or the way Dan hugged Nate and JR but he never told us to give him a hug. It was always just the usual handshake. But we were happy to see him. He asked us how we were doing and we said, "fine". He asked us to help him unload some stuff out of the car. He brought us a TV since we only had one TV in the house and it was in Rachel's room. He saw my mother and they spoke for a little while and then he left. We bid him goodbye with the usual handshake and said, "Bye, Popi." I always wondered what was going on in his mind. His family moved to Virginia and he was still in New York. Was he glad that we left so that he could attend to the business of the church or was he sad about it, and we just couldn't tell because he was able to mask his feelings really well? This is a question that we would never know the answer to.

After seven months of not being able to find a job, my mother decided to move back home to New York with my dad. She had given up on the dream of living the life that she was in search of and decided to go back to her husband and become the woman that he needed by his side and become the mother that her children so desperately needed her to be. Or so we thought. We didn't want to leave at all. We wanted to stay with Rachel, Mary and Dan. As usual our cries and complaints fell on deaf ears. The decision was made and we were on our way back to New York. Rachel drove us to the Greyhound bus station and it was a long ride back. No one spoke for the whole ride. Rachel was trying to cheer us up by telling us we could come back next summer but next summer seemed light years away. A day was too long, let alone next summer. My mother sat quietly in the front seat. Rachel used to take us joy riding in her car and it was fun. She would put on some classical music and just drive everywhere. She would drive for what seemed like hours. I smiled when I thought about the joy rides that she took us on, but my smiling soon turned to frowning as I realized that this was the last ride.

We waved goodbye to Rachel with tears in our eyes. She had tears in hers also. She was trying to wipe them away so we wouldn't see her crying but the tears were coming down so fast she couldn't stop it. My mother started to cry. I don't think my mother was crying because she was sad to leave, but she was crying because she saw how much we really wanted to stay.

Chapter Five

Back to Egypt

We were back in Brooklyn, and as soon I got there I wanted to go back. The roaches and the rats disgusted me, and the crack heads on every street corner didn't help either. My father was staying in this small apartment on east 35th Street in Flatbush. The rooms were pretty big, but my brother and I still had to share a room. The only thing about the apartment that everyone hated, not just me, was the kitchen. The kitchen was the size of a closet. It was so small we couldn't even fit a kitchen table in there. Trust me, we tried. We thought that maybe things would be different. But, they weren't. My father still wasn't talking to us and the only time he did speak was when he was arguing with my mother or when we got into trouble. It was weird. My adolescent mind couldn't comprehend the love stories that I continuously saw on TV, with the love that I saw Dan give to his children and his wife, in comparison to the deafening silence that my father allotted to both of his sons, topped with the reenactments of the L.A. Riots between my parents. One day my father was coming home from work and I looked outside the window and saw him coming out of his car. I yelled out the window, "Hi Popi," and he ignored me. That was weird I thought. When he got upstairs he yelled at me for doing that. I thought maybe it was some weird thing that I couldn't understand but maybe one day when I got older I would understand it, but I still don't get it. It was like he was taking his frustration out on us. My mother was still doing her partying and every Friday she took us over to her friend Diane's apartment so she could watch us. Diane didn't even watch us. Her daughter Shaniqua did. She was probably no more than 3 years older than us. Her apartment was always dirty and it always smelled like fried chicken. She lived in the projects and her door was never locked. I hated going over there. It was the epitome of the ghetto. The roaches didn't even run across the floor when the lights came on or try to scurry across the television screen while we were watching Married with Children, for fear of being stepped on .They just seemed to move as if they had just as much right as Diane and her daughter. The apartment was filthy. My mother would come staggering in all hours of the night and she would take us home in the morning. That was like our second home.

It was summer time and we went to my father's sister's house for the summer. My grandmother was there and so were my other 3 cousins. They were all girls; Marcy, Venice and Susan. My father's sister, or should I say my Aunt Gladys, married a man named Mono before she came to this country. He was a good, strong working man. They had a house in Irvington, New Jersey and that's where my brother and I spent our summers.

Jeffrey Barlatier

My grandmother, my father's mother, was like my mother. When she spoke we would listen. When my mother spoke we would hear. She showed us a lot of love when we got there. She would always pull us to the side and talk to us about what was going on with my parents. She would never go into detail but she would always stress how important it was not to let what was going on with them affect us. She would talk for what seemed like hours. She was the only one at the time that considered how we might have felt with everything that was going on with my parents. My grandmother was a very hard worker. Every morning she would get up at 5 or 6 and start her day off with prayer. She would then start washing clothes and cook breakfast for the entire house. My Aunt Gladys and Uncle Mono both worked in the city so they would ride down to Newark to catch the train together.

All of the kids, all five of us, would have fun during the summer, not going to the malls or playing video games till the wee hours in the morning, but doing something better. You guessed it, we would clean! We would clean till we cleaned every corner of the house. What still gets me is that no matter how much we cleaned, the next day it was messed up again! While all the kids across the street were riding their bicycles and playing jump rope we were painting and gardening. It wasn't that bad. They would let us ride our bikes and go to the park to play basketball, but only after the house was clean. Work first and play later, and did I forget to mention that we couldn't watch TV? That's right. The one thing that could link us together with all mankind was taken away from us. The television was off limits unless otherwise specified. They would make sure the television was far enough from an outlet so that we couldn't turn it on. My cousin Marcy, the oldest of the girls and the leader of the television revolt would find an extension chord that was plugged to something else and would go on secret missions to watch *Saved by the Bell* or *Selena* for the hundredth time. One time she even used the lights from the Christmas tree as an extension cord so that we could watch the TV. Christmas tree lights were just the beginning and if I were to go into all the devices we used I would be forced to dedicate an entire chapter just to our ingenuity.

Marcy was the only one that read books. I never read a book before then. She would always read books from the Goosebumps series. I had no passion for reading. I liked to just talk and joke around. Even in school I never read any books. When I had to write a paper for class on a certain book I would just read the back of the book and elaborate on it. I was so creative with words I would just make something up. What was ironic was that I won the school spelling bee but I never picked up a single book!

Summer at Gladys's house was fun. I loved being around them. They made us feel like family. They would take us on trips to Sesame Place and Great Adventure. Even going to get pizza was exciting with them. They made everything fun. Gladys and my grandmother were best friends and they talked about everything. We used to make fun of them because anytime we got into trouble with my grandmother we knew she would tell Gladys. We didn't want her to tell Gladys so we would beg her not to. She would tell anyway because they were best friends. I never heard Mono and Gladys fight. Not one time. They would call each other Cherie (French for honey) every time they spoke to each other. He never raised his voice at her and she didn't nag him like my mom nagged my father. I wonder if that's what my grandmother was talking about. She would always talk to us. Half of the conversations I don't remember but I do remember her washing dishes and her telling me and my brother to sit down at the table while she washed the dishes. I loved my grandmother. Mono was the ideal father, his girls loved him, and we loved him too. We never told him, but we did. Mono would always call my brother and me his two sons since he had all girls. It always made us feel good inside when he said that. He treated us like we were really his sons. But we still missed our father. The summer was winding down and it was time to go back home to Brooklyn. We stayed there all summer and it was time to go back.

Part III

Things started to change...

Chapter Six

Moving on up, to the Eastside

When we came back home for the summer my brother and I came home to find that my parents moved into another apartment. This time it was near Coney Island Avenue in Brooklyn. We lived next to the Pakistanians and the Jews so it was considered to be a good area. My brother and I still shared a room but we didn't see any crack heads when we went outside. It was a nice area. Maybe one or two roaches here and there, but nothing serious. We lived on the 2nd floor of a house. The landlord seemed like a pretty nice guy. He was Pakistanian and so was his wife. School was about to start and we were a little nervous. We lost count of how many schools we were new to by now. We felt like army kids. Every time we moved we left friends behind and were forced to find new ones. We walked to school the first day. When we first arrived at school we noticed that there was an epidemic going on with the kids at school that we weren't aware of. Everyone at the school was wearing name brand clothes but me and my brother. Well, everyone that was not a teacher that is. We didn't have any name brand clothes like the rest of the kids that were at school. Everyone wore Guess jeans, Tommy Hilfiger and Polo t-shirts. We had on the newest Fila sneakers but so did everyone else and they even had it in the newest colors which made our new sneakers immediately old. We had to keep our sneakers clean because we weren't going to get another pair until maybe January, and it was only September.

School was pretty cool. I was in the 6th grade and my brother was in the 7th grade. I made some friends as soon as I got to my homeroom class. Kyle, Anthony, Adam, Kyle Mason and McGregor were all in my homeroom class and they were funny. All of them were. We would throw paper and make jokes in class. My brother also made a few friends in his homeroom class. He was cool with this cat named Steve, who everyone knew because he was in the local gang called t.p.i. (true pimps international). Most of the gang went to the school and they were nothing to mess with. Everyone was scared of them.

From the very first day of school I fell in love with someone. I was a sucker for love. It was like love at first sight. Her name was Jennifer. She was Puerto Rican and was the finest thing I had ever laid my eyes on. From the first time I saw her I knew I had to have her. The only problem was that I didn't have any name brand clothes. Clothes were everything in school. Clothes were what defined you. It did not matter how funny I was, I needed some clothes to get the girls. I asked McGregor if he could try to hook us up since he went to elementary school with her. He went over to her and pointed me out to her. He didn't even have to tell me, because I saw her shake her head. He came back and said that she said, "no". I was heartbroken.

I tried out for the school band, for the position of lead drummer and I got it. I was happy about it because I was learning to play the drums at my grandfather's church. I was getting better and better each day. I liked playing for the school band. It was cool because Adam, McGregor, Anthony and Kyle Mason were all in the band with me. At least one of us got kicked out of class each week. We could not stop joking around. Everything was funny to us but when we played at our shows we were always serious. It was just at the rehearsals we would cut up.

There was this girl named Kathy that played the clarinet. She was Puerto Rican and I thought she was pretty cute. She didn't dress as good as Jennifer or look as good as her but she had a pretty smile and I had the feeling that she liked me. One day a fight broke out between her friend Cindy and my friend Kyle Mason. I was trying to hold him back but her friend Cindy was swinging at him really wild. I tried to step in between Cindy and Kyle, but I accidentally bumped into her friend and she fell into Kathy and they both fell on the floor. I tried to apologize to Kathy and help her up but she started cursing at me in Spanish and telling me she was going to get me beat up. I knew my chances of getting with her were pretty slim now but getting with her was the least of my worries. Kathy's best friend was Nikea and she was the leader of G.R.S. (girls run s*#@) and they were the girls that were associated with TPI. After school there was a whole mob of people walking towards my brother and me. We were trying to see who they were walking towards till we realized it was Kathy and her girls and half the 8th grade boys running towards us. My brother and I ran so fast, all they saw was dust. I never went back to that school again.

My mother's timing could not have been any more perfect. Her and my father were arguing every day again and she was tired of arguing with him. So she left. And again she took us with her. And again we returned to Virginia to live with Aunt Rachel. We were excited about going to live with Rachel again. But this time Rachel was married. She was married to a man named Daniel. Daniel was a nice guy. He was a little on the heavy side but he was a good man with a good heart. Especially since he was going to let us stay with him and Rachel.

Rachel and Daniel were newlyweds and were up for the task of letting my brother and I stay with them until my mother got on her feet. My mother brought us to Virginia but decided to leave after a couple of days. She went back to New York and left us with Rachel. Her plan was to save up enough money in New York with the job that she had up there and come back down with enough money to get an apartment down in Virginia. We didn't really care what the plan was. We were happy to be back in Virginia with Aunt Rachel. This time we even signed up for school so we were really looking forward to starting a new life in Virginia.

I joined the school basketball team and my brother joined the school football team. Everyone liked us, especially since there were so few blacks around. When they found out we were from New York they loved us even more. We were living the life. We had Nate and JR to hang out with and our other two girl cousins Jennifer and Crystal. Jennifer and Crystal were a year apart and they were around Nate's age. I loved them. They were hilarious. Crystal was the one that didn't like white people and Jennifer was the one that would beat anyone up, boy, girl, elderly, it didn't matter. I loved Jen, that's what we called her for short. They were like my big sisters. Everything felt so right when we were down there. We were getting good grades in school. Sometimes when Daniel and Rachel weren't around my brother and I would have girls over. We never did anything with them, well at least not me. I was still a virgin. We were just enjoying our adolescence.

Jeffrey Barlatier

One day I was home alone, John went out with one of his female friends and Rachel and Daniel were at work. I decided to watch a movie. DVD's weren't around yet so a VHS would have to do. I pulled out Poetic Justice but opted not to watch it since it would be my 12th time seeing it and I couldn't stand to see Chicago brushing his head again. Then I saw a tape that didn't have a label. I wondered what was on it. I put the tape in and pressed play. There was a little static across the screen and then I saw something that I never saw before in my whole 14 years of living. There was a naked black man on the screen kissing a white woman while he was playing with his penis. I wanted to close my eyes but I had never seen a white woman naked before, let alone a woman naked before. I kept my eyes on the woman but I couldn't understand why the black man kept moving his hand back and forth on his penis. He seemed to be enjoying it. This was the first time I had ever seen anything like it. I thought I heard a car door slam outside so I quickly took the tape out, put it where I could find it, and ran to the bathroom. I waited a few seconds and realized it was the neighbors that lived across the street from us coming home from work. As I sat on the toilet I couldn't get the images of the white woman and the hand motion that the man was doing to his penis, out of my head. No one had ever told me about the birds and the bees. I thought maybe that was how you were supposed to have sex. I decided that I would try to do the same thing that the black man was doing on the tape. I tried it for a few moments and it felt kind of weird. It was like I was scratching the inside part of my penis. I wanted to stop but it felt good. Really good. Thirty seconds later some white substance came out of my penis and I dropped to the floor. I didn't know what the white stuff was. I thought I had to go to the hospital. I was so scared the rest of the day; I thought I was going to die. I swore to myself that I would never tell anyone what I did in the bathroom that day. But the pictures of that naked black man and that white woman would stay with me for years.

Things were going well at Rachel's house. We were staying out of trouble and we were doing well in school. We hadn't heard from my mother in almost 9 months. It didn't bother us because we wanted to stay with Rachel forever. Then one day we got a call from my mother and she said that we would be moving again. My heart dropped and I threw the phone down and locked myself in my room. Why would she keep torturing us like this? I was tired of making new friends. And I didn't want to leave. We were happy. She told us that we were going to live with my grandmother at my father's sister's house in New Jersey. I wanted to go with my grandmother but I wanted to stay with Rachel. This time when we left, there were no tears. All the tear ducts in our eyes had dried up and we couldn't cry another tear. They say weeping endures for a night, but that night we wept, with no tears. We were luggage that my mother dragged around and she had no consideration for our feelings. We hated her for it. We never told her, but we did.

Chapter Seven

New Jersey Drive

When we got to my aunt's house everyone was glad to see us. We were glad to see them too. Marcy, Venice and Susan all embraced us and we hugged our grandmother with tears in our eyes. My grandmother looked both of us in the eyes and told us that God told her months prior that we would be coming to stay with her. She said that she dreamed we came running through the door breathing hard. When she turned around to ask us why we were breathing so hard. She said that we couldn't even catch our breath. After toiling day and night with what the significance of the dream was, she said that the Holy Spirit spoke to her and told her that my brother and I were tired of running.   We were tired of running from place to place. Moreover, that He was sending us to live with them so we can have rest. I remember the somber look in her eyes when she told us about the dream. I do not know if she was happy to see us or sad that we've been carried around like accessories. My brother and I were tired of moving. This was going to be our last stop.

After a few weeks we were off to school again. Only this time we were in Catholic school. We had to wear these shabby looking uniforms and had to take 2 busses to get there. The school's name was Citadel of Hope. It looked like an old monastery. We quickly made friends as soon as we got there. We were used to moving so much that we learned how to make friends on the first day of school. After two or three weeks at that school I got a girlfriend and so did my brother. My girlfriend was a little on the chubby side but I liked her because she had attitude. I mean she really had an attitude. She would tell anyone off, even me. She was cute and I liked her feistiness. She helped me with my school work and for the first time in my life I was getting A's and B's. In Virginia I was getting B's and C's but never any A's, those kinds of grades where alien to me. My aunt and uncle Mono didn't play when it came to education. That was the most important thing to them. Good grades were an expectation, not an option. They would give us 5 dollars for each A, 2 dollars for each B and a beating for any C's or worse. As a result no one got C's in that house.

It was getting close to graduation time. I was getting ready to graduate from the 8th to the 9th and my brother was going from the 9th into the 10th. Most of the students were only going to classes because their parents didn't want them to be at home doing nothing. Graduation was 6 days away, and the word around school was that a boy named Walter, who was a junior, was having a party at his house. Some of us decided to go. It was me, my girlfriend and a few of her friends that lived within walking distance of the school. The neighborhood that Walter lived in was really bad, it was somewhere in downtown Newark. When we got to the party Walter and all of his friends were there. My brother was there too. I went over to my brother to say 'what's up' and he couldn't even look me in the face. His breath smelled like liquor and he couldn't even stand up straight. I asked Walter what happened to my brother and he just pulled out this big water bottle filled with Cristal. I was pissed. I knew Walter was a trouble. I hated the fact that every time we moved my brother would always hang with the knuckleheads. My brother kept telling me that he was o.k. but he couldn't even walk straight. I put his arm around my shoulder and started walking toward the door. One of the boys that was in my brother's class was running around the house pulling everyone's pants down (pause). So as we were walking out the door he tried to pull my pants down. I told him to get off of me, and he wouldn't listen. He still tried to pull them down and I was yelling for him to get off of me. Before I could yell at him again my brother got up from his drunken stupor and said to Aaron, "Word up, don't touch my brother." Everything suddenly stopped moving. It was dead silent in the room. Aaron said, "word, then throw your hands up." My brother put his hands up and so did Aaron. By this time the whole house was watching what was about to happen. It was like Tyson vs. Holyfield except Tyson was drunk and could hardly stand straight. They went around in a circle once. And then Aaron swung. Why did he do that? As soon as he swung my brother ducked and hit him with an uppercut. Aaron flew backwards like he was trying out for the matrix scene when Neo dodged the bullets. His shoe came off and all you heard was "ooooohhhhh", a whimper and a shout. Aaron was knocked out cold. I mean cold. He wasn't waking up for anybody. We might as well have given him a pillow. Someone ran over to him and said "Aaron you got knocked the..." (You know the rest) I told my brother we had to get up out of there. I kissed my girlfriend goodbye and we left. I had to practically carry my brother to the house. When we got there he went straight to our room and went to sleep. I told my grandmother that he had a really bad headache and he slept for the whole night. That was the first time I saw my brother drunk, but it wasn't the first time I saw him knock someone out for me. He didn't fear anyone.

Both of my parents came to the graduation and that surprised me. Everyone was happy that day. After the graduation I went up to my father and I told him that I loved him. I don't know what made me do it. I just said it out of nowhere. This was the first time I ever said it to him and this was the first time he ever said it to me. I hugged him and it felt kind of awkward, but it felt good at the same time. My parents were proud of me and it made me feel good that they were. The whole family went to my aunt's house for a "Thanksgiving feast" that my grandmother cooked. She made chicken, fish, potatoes, rice, broccoli, macaroni and the list went on and on. I was so stuffed. I fell asleep and didn't even notice when my parents left.

The next day my mother called and told my grandmother that she wanted to talk to us. My brother picked up one phone and I picked up the other line. Her first words let us know that our lives as we knew it were doomed again. The first thing she said was "I know you guys don't want to leave but…" as soon as she said that I threw down the phone and went downstairs. She was doing it again. She wanted us to move with her to Long Island with her dad. I didn't want to go. The church was flourishing and her dad, now a Bishop bought a big house in Long Island. I went to my brother and saw him with tears in his eyes and with the phone glued to his ears. He didn't say a word; he just let the tears roll down his eyes. My cousins ran up stairs wanting to know what happened. When I told them they all started crying also. "Why, why would she do that?" they asked. I didn't know why. My mother was messing up my life and she seemed not to care. Two days later my mother drove up with a female friend and we loaded up our bags.

We didn't have much to pack. That night was the hardest night of my life. That was the first time I ever saw my grandmother cry. All I could think about was the dream that she told me she had. We were running again and we were tired. There was nothing we could do about it. We kissed our cousins goodbye and they all had tears in their eyes. My grandmother told us to be strong and not to let this affect us. She reminded us that we could come to visit her in the summer. I didn't want to let my grandmother go. My mother stood by the door of the car like she was getting irritated because we were taking so long. None of my cousins said "hello" or "goodbye" to her. She was the enemy.

Chapter Eight

Long Island Iced Tea

The ride to my grandfather's house was about 3 hours. When we pulled up to the house, I thought we were in the wrong neighborhood. The house was humongous. I mean huge. My grandfather was happy to see us. He hugged and spoke to us in Creole. He told us that he missed us and that he was glad that we came. As soon as I walked inside the house I asked my mother to use the phone. I called my grandmother and told her that we arrived at the house. I told her that I missed her and I wanted to come back. She told me to hang in there. I told her I loved her and I would call her back. The first thing that I liked about the house was that it was the first time that my brother and I got our own rooms. The house was so big we could have had our own floors. I never lived in a house that big before. My mother made us many promises that night. She told us that she was sorry for moving us around so much and that this was the last time we would have to move. We tried to believe her but she said that every time we moved. She promised that it would be different this time.

We attended the local school it was called Malverne High school. It was a pretty good school. The school was highly integrated and all of the white kids that went to the school lived in Malverne or in Lynbrook which was a nearby town. All of the black kids that attended the school were from Lakeview, which was another nearby town. I made a few friends my first day as, usual. And of course my brother hung out with the knuckleheads.

We were doing pretty well at the school. Our grades were decent, but there weren't A's and B's like when we were living in New Jersey. After a while we even got over the fact that we weren't living with our grandmother anymore. I wanted to live with her but my mother gave us a lot of freedom. I could go play basketball whenever I wanted. My mother gave me a curfew and an allowance. Things were going pretty good. I was on the junior varsity team and I was even allowed to practice with the varsity team as well. At night I would go and shoot around and practice in the park. I had big dreams of playing NBA basketball. I would eat, sleep and live for basketball and all the other kids I was hanging out with had the same aspirations. There would be times when I would go to the park and shoot around for hours. It would be 11 or 12 at night and my brother would be there with his friends, either high, drunk or both. Some of them would come on the court but my brother would tell them to leave me alone while I practiced. My brother wasn't the biggest one in the crew or the strongest but he had the biggest heart and everyone respected him for it.

I was doing pretty well at school. I had a lot of friends there. One day I went to lunch with some of my friends and we walked to the local store that wasn't too far from the school. All of my friends went inside the bagel shop and I went into the deli next door to order a chicken cutlet. I saw one of the girls from my social studies class named Dana. I always thought she was pretty. I had plans on trying to talk to her but, for some reason I didn't. I wanted to though. The timing had to be right. She was talking to a girl when I walked into the store, and I said, "Hey Dana, what's up?" The girl that was with her turned around and said, "Don't you see me talking?" When I saw her face whatever she said meant nothing to me. She looked gorgeous. I mean gorgeous. She was brown skin with, long black hair and a banggging body. I would usually have something smart to say, but I didn't. I just looked at her. Then Dana and the mystery girl walked out. This girl took my breath away. I went next door and asked my friends who was the girl that was walking with Dana? One of my friends ran outside and came back and said that it was Natasha. Natasha, who was that? She was a freshman at our school and everyone said was the prettiest girl in school. There was no argument from me. She was the prettiest girl I'd ever seen. Natasha was on my mind for the rest of the day. And the next day and the next. I had to say something to her. I just had to.

After days of trying to plan the perfect strategy of how to say something to Natasha I was forced to resort to romance 101, a letter. I know it was a chicken way to tell someone what you felt about them. However, I was hoping she found it a little bit more appealing than the other methods some of the guys were known for using. I hoped she considered it a better strategy than the one the guys were using, "Hey, what's up, Shorty?", or "Hey, ma, let me holla at you." Or the new one that was sweeping the hood, "pssssssssssssssssssssssstt", and calling to girls as if they were rattlesnakes or a tire going flat.

After that time I saw Natasha in the store I kept seeing her everywhere. I saw her between each class and I would make sure she saw me. I would go out of my way just so that she could see me walking by. I wasn't by far the flyest guy in the school but I looked decent. I always had on nice clothes and people were attracted to me because I was funny. I knew everyone and I was always walking with a girl through the hallways, even if they were just my friend. But none of them had anything on Natasha. She was badddd. I mean baddd. It was 7th period and we had two more periods to go before school was over. I wrote on a loose-leaf sheet of paper, "Why don't you stop talking to them corny cats and come talk to somebody real. I'm feeling you". It was corny but it was real. All of the guys in the school were trying to get with her and she wasn't giving anybody any play (attention). I felt like she was waiting just for me. The bell rang for 8th period. As soon as I walked out the classroom I saw her standing near one of the lockers. I said, "Hey you got some candy,"(she had a pack of starburst in her hand) she said, "Yea," smiled and handed me a purple starburst. I said, "Thanks!" and handed her the letter, turned around and walked away. I didn't know what to think. Would she find it corny? Or would she like it? I hoped she didn't read it   in front of everyone and make fun of me. For the whole 8th period class I sat silently as I heard each tick of the schools clock go by. Tic toc tic toc, I felt like I was going to explode. As soon as the bell rang, she was standing outside of my classroom with a letter in her hand. It was the same letter I wrote to her. She handed it to me and walked away. I watched her as she walked away. Her body was the shape of a Coca Cola bottle. I almost melted right there. She handed me the letter and I went into my class with the letter in my hand. Not knowing my fate, I opened the letter and these were the words that she wrote back "that was cute☺ you made me smile. Call me" She gave me her number and it took me a second to realize that I wasn't dreaming. She really just said what she said, or wrote rather. She found it cute. Romance 101 always works. Wow, I could have tattooed the number to my hand. I was excited and I couldn't wait to call her.

I planned on calling her as soon as basketball practice was over. I gave it my all that day at practice. I ran harder and I played harder. As soon as practice was over I called her from the school's pay phone. It rang twice, then an older male voice picked up. I asked if I could speak to Natasha and he asked for my name. I told him and I heard him call her to the phone. Later I found out that it was her grandfather and he wasn't too fond of boys calling for his granddaughter. When she came on the phone I was so nervous. I asked her what she was doing and she said nothing. We spoke for a few minutes but there was a lot of noise in the background. She asked me what I was going to be doing later. "Later," I thought to myself. It's 9 o'clock on a Thursday night. I usually went straight home after practice. I told her I didn't have any plans and she told me that she would meet me at the corner of my block at 12 midnight on the dot. I said, "Okay," but I was kind of confused. Where were we going at 12 midnight? It really didn't even matter. I had the "baddest" girl in the school on the phone and now I had a date. It was my first date.

I got off the phone and floated all the way home. I took a nice long shower and laid down on my bed. My adrenaline was pumping so I didn't have to worry about falling asleep. From my bedroom window I could see the corner of my block. The digital clock didn't seem to be moving fast enough for me. I wanted to do some pushups so I could look a little more muscular when she saw me, but that would mean I would have to take another shower. I went into my brother's room to kill time but he wasn't there. He had already snuck out. He snuck out every night of the week. My mother would go to sleep around 9 o'clock so after that my brother would go out the back door because it didn't make too much noise. My grandfather rarely stayed at the house because he wanted to be closer to the church. By this time the church was going through some changes because my mother's mother had passed away and my grandfather got married not too long after. The woman he married was from a catholic background and was much younger than him. I thought the woman was nice but others in my family thought otherwise. The church was splitting and all of the founding members had left. The only ones left were my dad and my grandfather. My grandfather believed that it was my father's fault that the members left but in all actuality it was his fault. The founding members, my father and my grandfather formed a council in which they made all of the decisions together-unanimously. The council members warned my grandfather that he shouldn't get married so soon, but he didn't listen. He wasn't used to being alone, let alone tending for himself. Members of the church began to leave because his getting married so soon after my grandmother died seemed a little shady.

One day my grandfather's new wife said that she thought the church would look better with a huge cross with Jesus hanging on it behind the pulpit. All of the members disagreed and they unanimously voted not to put up any graven images in the house of God. However, my step grandmother (who grew up catholic) believed strongly that it was necessary, the council still voted against it. "We are not Catholic" they declared, "we are Pentecostal and we don't have graven images in the sanctuary or in our homes". Guess what my grandfather did? You guessed it; he bought the cross anyway, and put it behind the pulpit. The council left, the congregation dispersed and the only one left standing there by his side was my father. It was sad to see how the mega church that my grandfather once pastored, that on any given Sunday would have 8-10,000 members was now reduced to 16 members that still believed that the church could be revived. Unfortunately, it never was. Members of the council planted other churches around Brooklyn but their ministries never reached the climax that my grandfather's church once had. Together they impacted many, but apart they impacted few.

Well, back to the date. It was around 11:55, and when I looked up the block, there she stood. It was dark outside but she looked like an African goddess. I don't even remember walking down the steps. I just kind of floated. Her hair was long and it was covering some of her face. That made me want her more. The 'Aaliyah look' was in, and she was killing it. I asked her where we were going and she said for a walk. Cool with me. We walked and talked, and talked, and talked. We walked until we found ourselves in the school football field at the top of the hill. We decided to sit down and talk and that we did. It was a little cold outside so she let me put my hands inside her shirt. I kept my hands on her stomach but I really wanted to touch her luscious breast soooooooooooooo bad... I could hear them calling me, but I didn't. I didn't want her to think I was like the rest of them. We talked for hours. It was 6 in the morning and we were still talking. It felt like we were playing catch up. As we walked I asked her if I could have a kiss. She leaned over and kissed me. It was the best kiss I ever had. Our tongues danced to music that wasn't playing. We were both on cloud nine. She told me she knew I was a good kisser, I laughed. She had so effortlessly boosted my ego with that one. I couldn't believe I was with one of the prettiest girls in Malverne and she just kissed me, and told me that it was good kiss. I walked her all the way home and gave her another kiss good night. After making out for 10 minutes I went home. I was in Utopia. I never experienced this feeling that I was having. I didn't even know what it was called but whatever it was; I didn't want it to end. I closed my eyes and all I could see was us walking, holding hands, sitting in the field and kissing. She had me open and I didn't care.

I woke up two hours later, and it was time to go to school. I was dead tired but I wouldn't take a single hour from last night back. I went into my brother's room to tell him what had happened but he wasn't there. When my mother came in and asked where my brother was I told her he left early to go to study hall. I told that lie a lot for my brother. He would spend the night at his boy's crib partying, drinking and smoking. By this time he had stopped going to school all together. He went from being late to school, to cutting a class or two, to cutting school, to just not even going. The only time he would go was when all of his friends went up to the school after school to check out the girls or recruit some of the younger boys from the neighborhood. Some of my friends at school grew up with my brother's crew so they would show me and my friends love and say what's up to us after school. You were counted among the cool kids if they acknowledged you in front of everyone. It was like you were one of them, even if you weren't.

Part IV
Things fall apart...

Chapter Nine

My Hobby, My Girlfriend and I

Natasha and I continued to see each other every night, at the same time for almost two weeks. We made out every night and I loved it. After about two weeks we were officially going steady (she was my girlfriend) and the whole school knew it. When we walked down the halls, I would have my arm around her and all the guys would be staring. I could imagine what they were thinking. How did he get her? I didn't even know. I was just enjoying the experience. She would come to all of my basketball practices and I would walk her home afterward.

The first time we had sex was the first time I ever had sex before in my life. No one knew that but her, and you. I told her in advance because I didn't want to look stupid if I messed up or didn't perform like a pro. She told me that she had only been with one person before me and that made me feel a little insecure because she could base me off of her previous experience. But when I thought about it, it didn't matter because I had her now. That was all that mattered. When we first had sex I used a condom and I climaxed in about 30 seconds, if that long. It was the best feeling in the world. It reminded me of the tape I found in my aunt's house and what happened to me in the bathroom. I liked this sex thing. It was new to me. We did it every night or any chance we had. We would sneak into my house and do it while my mother was silently sleeping across the hall. I snuck into her house and we did it there too. But we had to be really quiet because her bed would squeak and make lots of noise.

One night we was so into it we didn't care how much noise we were making. Her mother's room was downstairs and she heard us. She came upstairs and knocked on the door. I ran into the closet butt naked and she opened the door for her mother. Her mother asked what was that noise and Natasha, faking like she was just awakened from sleep said, "what noise?" Her mother walked right to the closet and started feeling around to see if someone was there. I tried to move back and duck but it was too late. The next thing I knew was that I felt her mother's hand touch my penis. She yelled for me to come out of the closet and I told her I couldn't because I didn't have on any clothes. Then I heard her grandfather ask what was going on in there. He came into the room and so did her grandmother. I just stood there in the closet. I was so embarrassed. I had never been this embarrassed in my life. They gave me my clothes and waited for me to get dressed. When I came out the closet, they were all there. I just put my head down and walked out of the front door. I was so embarrassed. But that didn't stop us. We had sex every opportunity we got. It was like a new hobby for me.

I knew we were supposed to be together forever. Her birthday was the day before mine! Could you believe that? My birthday was January 10th and hers was January 9th. We celebrated our birthday together every year. Going on our second year of being together Natasha told me that she wanted us to do something different for our birthdays. I asked her what and she said she wanted us to smoke some weed together. "Weed?" I looked at her like she was out of her mind. I didn't smoke weed and neither did she or so I thought. I told her no. She said ok and didn't bring it up again.

However, for some reason I couldn't get the thought out of my head. My brother and his friends were doing it and even some of my friends were. But that's no reason to do it, I thought. It was something different and she wanted to do it. I told her that I changed my mind and that we could do it on her birthday. The day of her birthday came and all of my friends knew what we wanted to do. It was like a ceremony when I think about it. I was classified as the good boy and my brother was classified as the bad one, so when I told my brother and my friends I wanted to do it they suggested that we come and do it with them. I said sure. We were over by our friend Omar's house and my friend Javon lit the blunt. I hated the smell but I dealt with it. Natasha didn't seem to mind at all. She had smoked before she met me so this wasn't her first time but it was her first time since she was with me. At least that's what she said. It was my first and last time I told myself. When it was my turn to smoke I didn't know how to inhale the smoke. Everyone was trying to show me but I couldn't do it. I just kept blowing the smoke out the front end of the blunt. Everyone just started laughing. I passed the blunt and waited for it to come around again. It was puff, puff then pass. If you took more than one puff you were called greedy and they skipped you when it came back around. So I finally took one good puff and I hated the way it tasted. I told them that I had enough and they laughed. They smoked

3 more blunts before the night was over. I didn't feel high that night. Not high at all. I went straight home and took a shower because I couldn't stand that awful stench. It smelled bad. I couldn't tell if Natasha was high that night because her hair was covering her eyes.

After that night Natasha and I decided to try it again. We brought our own bag from one of our friends at school and we got someone to roll it up for us, because we didn't know how to roll up a blunt. This time I got high. It felt a little weird at first but after a few minutes I felt like I was floating. Everything suddenly became funny to me. Natasha and I started laughing for no reason. We were having a good time. From that day on we smoked together every day. When we would sneak out and go over each other's house, before we went in we would smoke a blunt together. Then we would go inside and have sex. I was having fun and now I understood why my brother smoked every day. When I was high I wouldn't think about my problems. I wouldn't think about my dad or my mom. It was just me and Natasha.

I started cutting classes then eventually cutting school. I would either hang out with my brother and his friends, and Natasha or my best friend Sean at his house. I hung out with Sean the most. We were best friends. He played basketball and so did I. He liked to go to parties and dance and so did I. He was a better dancer than me though. As a matter of fact, he was the best dancer in town. We would both get high and just start dancing. He would do something and I would try to do the same thing until I got that move down pat. When we would go to parties we would get high and go in the party and set it off. Every time we went to a party everyone knew we were going to do our thing. They would automatically make circles around us and we would be the life of the party. Everyone wanted to dance like us. They would even steal our moves.

One day Sean and I wanted to smoke some weed but nobody had any. He said that he knew someone that always had weed and it was good weed. He called him D and in fifteen minutes the guy was outside. He hopped out of a gold 1998 Maxima. You could see that this cat was a real baller. His chain was hot and he had a big pinky ring on. He had the newest guess jeans on with a polo T-Shirt. He even had on a pair of Versace glasses. Sean introduced me to him and I gave him dap (hi-five, handshake) He seemed like a cool cat. Ever since that day I only bought weed from him.

We would talk here and there. I didn't have any money and I wasn't going to school, and all I was doing was smoking all day so I saved up some money and bought a half ounce of weed from D. I sold the whole thing in one day. I called D that night and bought an ounce. It took me 2 days to sell the ounce. I took the money from that and flipped it. I flipped it again and again and again and again. I didn't stop. I was started making $ 1,400 -$1,800 dollars a week just selling weed. Once I saw how much money I was making, I decided I definitely wasn't going back to school. D and I got real cool. At first I thought he liked me because I was making him money but then he told me that I was trustworthy. I hung out with him every day. We became best friends. He even took me on trips to the Bronx to buy some more product. Sometimes D would feel a little skeptical about picking up the product from the Dominicans because there were so many cops walking around on the streets, so he would give me $300 just to walk from the door to the car. $ 300 was nothing to him. He would spend that in one day on food. He would park a few blocks away so I would have to do a little walking, but I wasn't scared. Not one bit. I would be high the entire time.

One time we went to pick up some coke (D sold weed, crack, and coke) and some hydro (a strong type of marijuana) in the Bronx, from the Dominicans. I told the lady behind the counter I wanted some Hydro and she pulled it out of a brown paper bag that was in the garbage can near the bathroom. I bought $4,300 worth of hydro. The profit I was going to make on that was going to be ridiculous because I was going to make more than double. D was nervous about walking out with the product so he told me he would give me $300 to bring it to the car. He wasn't getting a good vibe. I said, "Cool." He told the Dominicans to give it to me. They handed it to me and I went inside the bathroom. The bathroom was next to the garbage can so while their heads were turned I snatched the brown bag that was in the garbage can that had the Hydro in it. I put the weed and the crack (cooked up coke) in my jacket and walked out the front door. I was a little scared because there was a few cops around the corner. I walked to the car and we were out. We were on our way back home I told D that I stole the hydro from the Dominicans. He was a little upset at first but then he shrugged his shoulders and started to laugh about it. I rolled up some of that hydro and started smoking. A few minutes later, all I heard was the whoop whoop of police sirens. We looked into the mirror and it was the cops. D was scared out of his mind, and for the first time I was scared too. D pulled over and the cops asked us to step outside the car. They smelled the weed smoke as soon as we got out. The officer asked who was smoking in the car. We told him we weren't smoking in the car; it was someone we just dropped off that was smoking. He looked at D and said, "Why would you let someone else smoke in your car if you don't smoke?" D told him that it was his little brother and that his brother doesn't listen to him; he does whatever he wants. The cop could tell it was a lie, but there was nothing he could do. Before I got out the car I had already stashed the product under my chair, so I didn't have anything on me. The cops talked for a few seconds and then let us go. I'm not sure why he didn't search the car but I was happy he didn't. D used to carry 2 guns in his trunk: a 22 caliber for the small problems and a 357.Smith & Wesson for the big ones (pause). I didn't think he had the heart to use one of them but he knew I did. I was hustling, riding around with guns and making money. And I liked it, I was having fun. My clothes were always fresh, and I always had a new pair of sneakers and money. One night I made $ 3,400 selling weed, in one night! I tried doing the crack thing but it wasn't really working. Most of the customers were D's and I wasn't trying to move in on his territory. We had an agreement. He stopped selling weed and sent people to me if they wanted to buy and anyone interested in crack or coke, I sent them to him. He hooked me up with his connect so I started buying weed by the pounds. But when I bought my first ton I thought I was never going to sell all of it. But it was all gone in a matter of weeks. We were living the life.

One night, I was walking down the block to my house and I noticed a dark unmarked car sitting in front of it. I knew it was the d's (detectives, not to be confused with my friend D) because of the kind of car and I didn't have too many white friends. In fact, I had none. I knew I didn't have any money or weed on me. I left the money under my girlfriend's mattress and the weed in a stash house that D and We had around the corner from my girlfriend's house. I left my money under my girlfriend's mattress so that my mother wouldn't find it if she ever decided to look through my stuff. I knew my girlfriend would take some cash here and there but she didn't know that I knew. I kept walking and wondering what they were doing there. As I came closer to the house, two men jumped out of the car and asked if my name was John. I replied, "Who are you?" "Are you John?" They asked, as they came closer to me. I said, "Who are you?", defiantly now. The two men grabbed me up and slammed against the car. I started cursing and swearing and then my mother came running out of the house saying, "That's not him! That's not him." The d's let me go and I was still cursing. I went inside the house and asked my mother what was going on. The officer walked in behind me and said, "We know you and John did it, so you might as well confess now." "Confess to what?" I said. Supposedly my brother was connected to a string of burglaries that happened in the town next to us. On one occasion the thieves made off with more than $15,000 in cash and jewelry. The d's said there were 2 sets of finger prints. They knew the first set was my brothers because he had beaten up this cat that cut me a few months back and he was taken down to the precinct and finger printed. All of the questions that I could have asked myself to question why my brother would do such a thing, or why didn't he just come to me for money, he knew I had it, were nowhere near my frame of thinking. "Why didn't he use gloves?" I said to myself.

They told me that I might as well confess because they were pretty sure that the other set of finger prints were mine. I told them that they weren't and I went into my room and shut the door. I paged my brother 911 and waited for him to call me back. I could hear my mother crying from my room. As I was sitting on the bed I heard one of the officers outside my window say, "We got em!" By the time I looked out the window my brother was being handcuffed and pushed inside the unmarked car. One of my friends who was with him before they handcuffed him said that he came running down the block because he heard that some cops were trying to arrest me, not knowing that they were really there for him. This was the one time that my brother came to my rescue, not knowing he would be the one needing the rescuing. I had enough money to bail him out but the judge didn't set a bail. Even if they did set it, my mother would definitely want to know where I got the money from. Up until this point I was able to hide from her the fact that I was hustling. I called D and told him what had happened and he was at a lost for words. He came and picked me up and I smoked 2 blunts in his car by myself. D never smoked. He would sell it but he wouldn't smoke it. My brother never told the d's who his accomplice was but we all knew who it was. My brother hung with a lot of people but he had one main friend that he was always with and he was nothing to mess with.

Chapter Ten

Up North

We got my brother a good lawyer. The lawyer was able to get the judge to seal his records so that if he ever looked for a job, no one could see that he had a felony charge previously. Unfortunately, even though it was his first time, he was in Nassau County and they didn't play. They sentenced him to 1-3 years. He could have just gotten probation but since he didn't want to tell the detectives who the other person was, they gave him time. My brother was being taken away from me and there was nothing I could do about it.   My brother didn't tell me much about jail except that it was hard and that you could die. He would call every now and again and I would tell him how much I missed him. We'd been through everything together, and this was the first thing that he was going through alone. I was devastated, my best friend, my brother was gone.

The prison experience was also hard on us. My mother took it really hard. Every night she would cry. She would go see him every weekend faithfully but when she came home from those 10-12 hour bus trips to the prison, she would be tired. The fatigue wasn't even from the trip but from the constant crying she had done. She blamed herself for him being in prison, and we blamed her too. Why didn't she just leave us in New Jersey? Or in Virginia? By now I was smoking 3 blunts a day by myself and drinking. I was still hustling but not like before. More and more people started selling weed so it made it more difficult to hustle in the same neighborhood as them. I started doing other things to get money. I started doing robberies by myself. I didn't need anyone telling on me. I didn't even tell D what I was doing. By this time he was like my Dad and I didn't want him being upset with me. One time I made off with $11,000 from one store. It took me 5 minutes to get $ 11,000. Without my brother there it, was like life lost its value. D would hold me down though (took care of me). He would always talk to me about doing other things with my life besides hustling. I was still with Natasha but even she missed my brother. Some days we would just hold each other and cry. It was like he died and the world was just moving on.

Chapter Eleven

D

One day I kept calling D and he wouldn't answer his phone. He always answered his phone. The only time he didn't answer was when he was with his girlfriend, Shay. I would call her phone and she would answer, and then put him on the phone. Shay was his wifey (main girlfriend). She looked good and she was high maintenance. D kept her in Gucci, Moschino and all the hottest name brands. But on this specific day, I called Shay and she didn't answer her phone either. That was strange. I was at my girlfriend's house, so I told her lets walk up to the store, maybe we'll see him up there. He didn't hang out over there but most of his customers did.

I decided to wait outside of Natasha's house as she got ready to take the walk with me. As I was waiting my boy Julius came outside of his house. He lived next door to Natasha. He walked up to me and gave me a pound (another word for hi-five). He said, "Hey you heard what happened to D?"

I already knew what he was talking about because a week ago D was arrested for having some coke in the back of his car and he was out on bail. I told Julius, "It ain't nothing. He's gonna get a good lawyer and beat the case." I looked at him and he was giving me a strange look.

"Nah, man. Not that. You aint hear, D got murdered?"

I said, "D who? Not my D. I was just calling him."

He said, "Yes, Jeff, your D!"

I started laughing because clearly he was mistaken. My girlfriend came walking outside and she said, "Baby, what's wrong?"

I said, "Julius tell Natasha, what you just told me."

He told her that D got murdered. "Word is bond (I'm telling the truth)." He said. She looked at him like he was crazy. We walked away from Julius because he had to be bugging out. I decided to walk to D's mother's house that was a few blocks away. His little brother lived there and if something like this did happen he would know. But I was sure that Julius was talking about the wrong person. But the look on his face scared me. By the time I got to the corner of his mother's house, there was a large crowd of people in front of her house. As I was walking through the crowd, everyone was looking at me. I kept saying to myself that this was a cruel joke and that it wasn't funny. But no one was laughing. They were just looking. I saw D's little brother sitting on the porch with Shay. He looked at me, and then put his head down. I asked if it was true. He looked up and it was like he didn't have enough strength to say it was. But the tears that were rolling down his eyes were confirmation. I walked away from the crowd. I couldn't believe it. I had to go somewhere and think.

People were calling my name but I just kept walking. If all of this was true then I had to get to the stash house (where we kept the money, drugs and guns). My money was in a safe and so was the weed. My girlfriend didn't even know how much money I had in there. I had to have close to $ 25,000 in the safe. As I was walking to the house, an unmarked car pulled up. They almost looked like the same detectives that arrested my brother. They called me by my name and told me to get into the car. I told them no and kept walking. Three white men got out and the one in passenger seat said, "Don't make me have to ask you again!" I saw the seriousness in his face and his hand slowly moving towards his gun. I got into the car and they took me down to the same precinct that D was held at. They interrogated me for 3 hours. They asked me if I knew who D's enemies were, or who would want to do something like this to him. They figured I knew, because by this time it was well known that we were best friends. I didn't know who would do something like this. But I remember this one run (drug delivery) we went on. There was this 'cat' that just came out of jail and everyone knew him. He didn't come outside much. But one day D told me to wait in the car while he made a drop .We pulled up in front of this house we'd never been to before. By this time I knew all the spots but this was a new one. It wasn't too far from the local store. D goes inside the house, handles his business and comes back into the car. Before I ask him anything he says, "Next time I go make a drop to that nigga, I'm gonna give you the gun and you gonna make the drop for me. I don't trust that nigga." I never heard D say that about anybody. I nodded my head and said, "Cool!" and we pulled off. I didn't tell the officers that, I kept it to myself.

The officers out of their frustration of me not being able to help them threw the pictures from the crime scene in front of me. It was D, dead. His face covered in gray and blood coming out of his mouth. His eyes were partially opened, and up until this very day I can't get those pictures out of my mind. The crime scene report said that D was robbed, beaten, handcuffed, shot 3 times in the back of his head, and burned in the trunk of his gold maxima. His car was found on the corner of 167th street in the Jamaica section of Queens, NY. Up until that very moment I thought this was all just a really detailed dream, but those pictures were real. The d's took me back to my house and as soon as they left I went to the stash house. I ran all the way there. I was still unable to get that picture out of my head. As soon as I got to the stash house the landlord came outside and told me that D's sister had already come to the house and taken the safe. I called her but she didn't answer. I thought about those pictures night and day. The affect of him being dead really didn't register until the funeral. Up until then I never cried. But as soon as I touched the doors of the funeral home tears started coming down my eyes. He was really gone. He was dead. I had no brother, no friend and no father.

The days seemed to roll into each other. By now I was always high and drunk. My life was meaningless at this point. I didn't want to live. There was no point. When my girlfriend told me a few days later that she was pregnant, she gave me something to live for. We decided that if it was a boy we would name him after D, in his memory. A month later, she had a miscarriage. Life just seemed like a series of minutes and hours that would roll into each other that led to nothing.

**Part V
Steady falling...**

Chapter Twelve

Switch

    My brother came home from jail and I was glad to see him. It felt like a piece of my life had come back. My brother was lifting weights in there so when he came out he was as big as a house. I mean he was humongous (pause). He had a different mindset too. You could see it when you were around him. He would always stay away from trouble. If you looked like trouble he walked away from you. He was still drinking but he wasn't hanging out like he used to and the guys he was hanging with respected that. I missed my brother. I was happy to have him back. Having him there made the loss of D a little easier but I missed D a lot. He didn't take the place of my brother; he took the place of my father.

Before my brother came home from jail, my mother moved to an apartment in Queens. She wanted to keep my brother away from all the "riff raff" that was going on in Long Island. We still would hang out there but not as much. My mother started going back to church when my brother went to jail, and I could see that she was changing. She didn't drink anymore and she didn't have any of her friends over to the house any more. This was the first time I had ever seen my mother go to church on her own. She didn't go to her father's church, but she was going to some church in East New York. We never asked her the name but whatever church she was going to, you could tell it was making a major difference in her life.

October 7, 1999 3:15 p.m.

I was sitting in the park playing spades with some of my former schoolmates. It was 70 degrees outside and it was a nice day. I saw my girlfriend walking up the hill with one of her cousins. She was crying so I knew something happened to her. I ran over to her and asked what happened, and she told me that she got into a fight with this girl named Keisha. Now Keisha was one of those ghetto hood rat girls the guys would never make their girlfriend but who was good enough for a one night stand. AKA Jump off. And that's exactly what she was to me. But my girlfriend didn't know that, at least I hoped not. She was crying so much I couldn't even get the whole story out of her.

Her cousin told me that Keisha was bragging that she had slept with me and my girlfriend overheard her so she swung on her. My first thought was, I knew she would tell. Before we even did anything I told her she couldn't say anything to anyone because if my girlfriend found out it would be trouble. She said, "okay" and we had sex that night. It only lasted about 15 minutes and it wasn't even all that. I knew I couldn't trust her. My girlfriend didn't believe her anyway but was mad that she was saying it, so she swung on her. I noticed on her face she had a few scratches. From the way her cousin was talking, it didn't sound like my girlfriend won the fight. That was a first. I knew my girlfriend knew how to fight, because we fought all the time, literally. But I was shocked to hear that Keisha grabbed her hair and punched her in the face numerous times. She got the best of her. I told her to wait at the park while I walked over to Keisha's house. I knew something like this would happen. I just knew it.

October 19, 1999 3:45 p.m

I knocked on Keisha's door and when she opened the door, she was smiling. This was all some big joke to her. I asked why she had to go and open her big mouth. She was laughing. That made me so mad. I told her how much I regretted sleeping with her and that it wasn't even all that. In fact it was the worst! She stopped laughing and called me every name in the book. She told me she was going to get her sisters boyfriend to come and kill me and I told her "bring it on". And it was on. Her sister's boyfriend was from Hempstead and was nothing to mess with.

October 19, 1999 4:10 p.m.

I walked over to Javon's house and knocked on his door. He lived maybe 4 blocks from Keisha. Javon was a known drug dealer around the way that was getting money. The main reason he was getting money was because D was his main supplier. After D's funeral he told me if I needed anything from him to let him know. And I needed something from him, and I needed it fast. I told Javon what I needed and he came out with it in a brown paper bag. I looked inside and it was a 22 caliber gun. It wasn't the biggest gun in the world but it could get the job done. I walked over to my girlfriend's house and told her that I would be gone for a few hours. She knew I had a gun on me and she told me to be careful. Everyone in town knew about the beef that I had with Keisha and everyone was looking to see what would happen. News about beef (trouble, war) traveled fast. I went to the corner store and waited. Bring it on I said to myself.

October 19, 1999   5:48 p.m

    I smoked 2 blunts by myself and shared one with my boys that were with me at the corner store. The corner store was where most of the people from Lakeview hung out. That afternoon, I wasn't sure how many people were up at the store because they wanted to see what was going to happen, but there were quite a few people there. Around 7:30 I was the only one left at the store. I figured   everyone went home to get dressed for whatever parties or clubs they were going on that night. Whatever the reason, I knew it wasn't wise for me to be standing in front of the store as an open target. But, on the other hand I was determined to prove to everyone I wasn't no chump so I stood right in plain view and nothing would happened. The gun was just in case my plan didn't go accordingly.

October 19, 1999 9:07 p.m.

    After standing in front of the store for a while I saw a green Lexus pull up. I started to reach for the gun until I recognized the face. The door opened. I was surprised to see Melissa hop out. "Whose car is that?" I asked while she gave me a hug.

"My mom's," she replied.

    I was chilling with Melissa in her mother's green Lexus that she left for her to take care of while she went to see family in Florida. Melissa had just gotten her license and her mother left her strict instructions not to touch her car. Of course she didn't listen. Melissa was one of the girls I went to high school with and she had a big crush on me. And I mean big. She asked me if I wanted to be her boyfriend but I told her I wasn't looking for a girlfriend at that time. That night, Natasha went and hung out with some of her female friends so I decided to hang out with my female friend, Melissa. I didn't feel like standing in front of the store anymore. There was nothing going on and Keisha's sister's boyfriend didn't show . We were driving down the main street in our neighborhood and we ran into my brother. He had a tank top on and he was looking real diesel. He spent his time wisely in jail. He was walking with Melissa's cousin, Preston. Preston was one of the craziest guys I had ever met. Both his parents had died in front of him when he was young and it caused him to have some huge anger issues. They both hopped into the car and we were on our way, where to? We had no idea. I asked if she wanted to drop my brother at home because he lived in Queens and she said sure.

We were driving down Hempstead Turnpike going towards Queens. We had the music blasting and Melissa was doing about 70 miles per hour. As we were driving we passed a car that had 4 girls in it and they all looked good. I signaled for them to pull over and they did. Melissa pulled over and she started backing up the car. So my brother and I jumped out the car. As Preston was getting out of the car, Melissa was still backing up. She didn't notice him getting out and she couldn't hear him over the loud music telling her to stop. The rear passenger door hit a telephone pole and bent backwards! I could hear Melissa screaming from down the block. We didn't even have time to talk to the ladies, we just ran back to the car to find the door barely hanging off the hinge. Melissa was crying and Preston was pissed. We tried to shut the door and it wouldn't even shut. It was finished. We got back into the car and headed towards my brother's house in Hollis, Queens with Preston holding the door the entire time. If he hadn't held it, it would've fallen right off. Melissa couldn't even talk, tears just kept rolling down her eyes. Her mother was going to kill her.

10:00 pm

    We dropped my brother off and we were headed back to Long Island. I was planning on sneaking into my girlfriend's house and spending the night there without her mother knowing. As we were driving down Jamaica ave. we noticed a cop van next to us. They were on Melissa's driver's side. The first thing that popped into my mind wasn't the door; it was the gun that I was still carrying. I told them the cops were right next to us and not to look suspicious. That was the wrong move because they automatically began to look more suspicious. The cops slowed down and pulled up behind us. That wasn't good. The cops noticed Preston holding the door and put on the siren. As soon as it came on I almost peed in my pants. I told Melissa not to stop the car because I had a gun on me. She started crying hysterically. I tried to throw the gun out the window but she was driving so slow they would have noticed it. I didn't know what to do, I wanted to get out of the car and just run, but they probably would've shot me. With the NYPD, you never know. I took the gun out of my waist and threw it under the chair. We stopped and 3 cops jumped out of the police van. The first cop asked Melissa for license and registration, but all she could do was cry. That made the cops more suspicious. "What's the matter?" the man asked her, and I noticed the female cop pointing her flashlight towards my feet. Please don't find it I thought to myself. All I heard was "step out of the vehicle". And that's all she wrote. We got out of the car and next thing you know we were all under arrest. This was just what I needed.

    At the station the cops frisked me and found 3 dime bags of weed and added that to the gun possession charge. They asked me whose gun it was and I said I didn't know and I didn't even notice it in the car. They threw me in the cell with a man that looked like a bum. The man was singing some old 70's song. He didn't even have a shirt on, so I noticed a few stab wounds and a bullet wound that he had on his upper body. When he lifted his head up to see who was in the cell, it was Old Dirty Bastard from the Wu-Tang Clan. Can you believe that? That was the funniest thing that happened to me all night. He didn't talk much but you could tell he was high on something and it wasn't weed. A detective pulled me into the interrogation room and told me to tell them whose gun it was. I told them I didn't know. They told me everyone in the car had told them it was mine and if I gave them a signed confession they would let me go. "Yeah, right!" I told the detective, "It's not my gun."

He said, "Okay," and sent me back to my cell.

In front of the judge was a blessing. The cells were crowded with people that committed from as petty an offence as hopping a turnstile, to those more heinous as murder. I was shocked to learn that Melissa had told the detectives that it really was my gun. Can you believe that? How did I know? The legal aide read a statement from her that said the words I repeated verbatim, "Don't stop the car, I got a gun in the car!" .We didn't even make it to trial, for God's sake we were in arraignment and she already telling! That really hurt my case. The judge set everyone's bail at $500, and set mine at $1,000. Even though Melissa told on me she still had to go to Rikers Island. She wasn't getting out any faster than I was. Our next stop, Rikers Island.

We arrived at Rikers Island with a bus load of criminals. Old Dirty bastard was bailed out from the court house. There were drug dealers, murderers, and prostitutes on the bus with us. They kept the women in the front of the bus and the men in the back. Preston and I didn't really talk much on the way there. I knew he was pissed but I was happy that my brother wasn't in the car when we got arrested. He would have been sent back to prison for violating parole. I figured we would be okay because Preston was one of the toughest guys in the neighborhood and though I wasn't the best fighter in the world, I could still hold my own. It might not be that bad I told myself. But I really didn't believe that. I was scared. We were taken off the bus and brought into the building C-74, the adolescent detention wing at Rikers Island. We were put inside a cell and left to wait until processing. There was an inmate there mopping the floors. He had to be in his early thirties. I called him over to our cell and asked him how it was there. He looked at me with a straight face and said, "Partner, its wild! Don't let anybody play you because if you do everyone will be playing you." He told me that the biggest thing with the adolescents were the gangs. The bloods had the most in numbers. He asked if we were in a gang and I told him "no" and he said, "that was good", and that we should stay like that. The more he talked the more I kept realizing where I was and what I had gotten myself into. I wanted to go home.

The officer opened our cell and told us to follow him. He brought us into a room and told us to strip down, totally. I thought he would leave while we were changing but he didn't. He stood right there watching. He had to be gay I thought to myself. He told each of us to step forward turn around spread our butt cheeks and cough (pause). He had to be kidding, but I soon found out he wasn't. He was dead serious. That was the most degrading thing I had ever done. I kept thinking this is just a bad dream, but it wasn't. This was real. He told us to put our clothes back on and he led us to where we would be sleeping. The dorm we slept in was called Mod 1. When we got there everyone was sleeping and it was quiet. I was expecting to be put in a cell but it was a dorm, like they have in the army.

If me and Preston could stick together we would be fine. The officer assigned each of us a
bed and we were 3 beds away from each other. I didn't want to go to sleep. "What if someone tried to rape me?" I thought. I had seen the show OZ many times and I didn't want to become anybody's girlfriend. As I laid there thinking about what a mess I got myself into, I fell asleep.

An officer kicked my bed and told me, "On the count." I didn't know what that meant, but I got up anyway. Each time a duty officer would come on to his shift he would count the inmates to make sure all were present. They called this count time. As soon as count was over, I washed my face, brushed my teeth and went to breakfast. If I could even call it that. The food was disgusting. The next couple of days were a blur. We really didn't do anything but watch TV, eat and sleep. I made my phone call to my girlfriend telling her to bail me out as soon as possible. She said that she was working on getting the money and she would have me out in a few days. I told her to ask my mom for a few bucks but she said she had already, and her response was that she should leave me in there. "Don't waste your money because he's going to go back in anyway". Natasha told me not to worry about it. She would get the money somehow and have me out in a few days. The dorm   house that we were in wasn't so bad. No one came up to us and bothered us and everyone was pretty much to themselves. I thought it would be worse.

Chapter Thirteen

Thug Life

One morning when I woke up someone told me that they moved Preston to another dorm. When I asked "why?", he told me that we were just in a holding dorm and that we were all going to get moved today. I figured wherever we were going would be like the house we were in. I was wrong. They moved me to a dorm that was located outside and they called it the sprungs. I don't know why they called it the sprungs but when I got there I wanted to go back to the other dorm. Everyone in that house was either a Blood or a Latin King. I could tell because they all had the 3 burn marks on their arms. The guys in there looked at me like they all had beef with me. And what made it worse was Preston wasn't even in the same house as me. I really had to hold it down by myself.

Out of everyone that lived in the dorm there was one person that ran that house. His name was Raw. You would think that the officers controlled the house, but actually it was controlled by the toughest guy in the house. And Raw was the toughest guy in the house. He didn't look so tough to me. But I wasn't trying to test him to see if he was. I just wanted to get bailed out and go home. The officer showed me to my bed and left. I felt like a child taken to school on the first day and his mom leaves him right in front of the school. Someone walked up to me and asked me what gang I was in and I told him I was neutral. He said, "Okay" and walked away. For the first couple of days no one really said anything to me. They just went about their daily routine and I just watched and waited.

One day while I was in the day room they had called for everyone to get on the count. I was so into the show that I was watching that I didn't hear them. I just felt one of the plastic chairs hit me on my head. When I turned around it was RAW. He looked me dead in the eye and said, "Nigga, I said on the count!" I looked around and everyone was waiting to see what I would do. I even saw some officers looking to see what my reaction would be. I looked him back in the eye and said "Aiight no doubt!" I got up and walked to my bed for the count. It was one of the worst things someone could have done. Now everyone would be looking at me like I was a punk. But all I wanted to do was go home with no cuts on my face or scratches or bruises. And if anyone knows anything about Bloods, they don't fight fair anyway. It would have been me and him initially, and it would have ended with me being stomped by 30 of his Blood brothers. I called my brother on the phone that night and he was upset with me for not doing nothing about it. "You don't let nobody play you," he said. I heard the anger in his voice when he said it. I told him I knew but Rikers is different from Nassau County Correctional (he did a year there before he was sent upstate). In Nassau County the correction officers ran the house but in Rikers, the inmates do. I've heard stories about inmates dying while being jumped by other inmates and the CO (correctional officer) just watching. He was quiet. He knew where I was coming from, and I knew where he was coming from. We hung up the phone and I went to bed. I hated this place. I wanted to go home.

It was going on two weeks and I still was in this hell hole. I called Natasha when I could because Raw was charging people to make phone calls. Rikers gave every inmate two free calls and one collect call. The free call was a 7 minute call that you got once a day. Any additional calls that you wanted to make, your family had to put money in your commissary so you could make those calls. Let me not forget, not only was he charging people who wanted to make one of their free calls, but he was also charging rent. Everyone that wasn't a Blood or a Latin King had to pay rent-a living fee. The fee was a box of chocolate chip cookies and a pack of cigarettes. It didn't sound like much but if there's 50 adolescents in the house and 20 are Blood, 10 are Latin King and the remaining 20 are neutral, it comes out to be 20 boxes of cookies, 20 packs of cigarettes, and 20- 7 minute phone calls every other week. Some of the inmates didn't agree with the policy that Raw imposed so they revolted. It didn't work though. The loud mouth was jumped the next day while he was sleeping and the others that didn't agree quickly had a change of heart.

One day I was sitting in the day room and I saw this kid with a shirt around his head with writing on it. The writing said ABG. I asked him what it meant and he said, "Anybody get it!" He was real short but he looked pretty tough and I asked him what his name was. He said, "Sean but everyone called him little ABG." I had never heard of that gang before, but he was repping it real hard. He was cool with all of the Bloods in the house and they all respected him. He asked me if I had a light and I said, "yea". I asked him if he could save me some of his cigarette and he said, "yea".

Now I had never thought about being in a gang before. And I knew I definitely didn't want to be a Blood or a Crip. I liked being neutral but it was the way that little ABG carried himself that made me want to be down. He was the shortest person in the house but he wasn't scared of nobody in there. He told me that he was a golden gloves champion for one year and that's how he learned to fight. He was from Brownsville and that's where the gang originated. The reason he was so cool with most of the Bloods was because ABG fought with the Bloods in the streets of New York against the Crips.

I asked what I had to do to get in the gang. He told me that I would have to fight him one on one. I asked if he was sure it would only be me and him fighting and no one else, and he said that it would only be him. "Let's do it", I said. We both went and put our boots on and then went into the bathroom, then we went at it. Having your boots on in jail was a sign that you were ready to fight. It was hard for me because he was short and fast, so I figured I could just lift him up and slam him. That was a bad move. He was pretty strong and he was getting the best of me. One of the officers ran into the bathroom and shouted for us to break it up. We told him we were just playing around and he left. We weren't even in there for 5 minutes and I was out of breath but Little ABG was ready to go for round two. When he saw that I didn't have a round two in me, he said, "Yo, you're in." He gave me five. My lip was a little swollen but it wasn't anything serious. He told me to follow him. He walked up to Raw with me standing behind him and he told Raw that I was down with ABG and if somebody had a problem with me they had a problem with him. Raw looked at me and asked him if we fought one on one. He said, "we did". Raw saw the bruise on my lip and said "okay". I felt like he was my big brother and he was going up to my school to tell everyone it was hands off when it came to me. This meant I didn't have to pay rent like everyone else or give up my phone calls. Little ABG did say that I would have to share my commissary with him because he didn't have anyone to put money in his account. That was fine with me. He didn't need any phone calls because from what he told me his mother was in the hospital sick and his girlfriend's phone was cut off. That day he made me a shirt with the same writings he had on his and he told me the ABG oath. I was to recite that oath every day and memorize it. He showed me the handshake that all ABG members did when they greeted each other. This was the first time I felt part of something. It was like someone had my back and I had theirs. I was in this gang for life.

The other inmates in the dorm looked at me a little different after they found out I was down with ABG. Me and little ABG did everything together and we watched each other's back. There was one incident when a Crip came into the dorm and was talking a lot of trash to little ABG and ABG swung on him. The kid fell to the ground and I jumped in and we stomped him out. I think that was the occasion when everyone knew I took this gang thing seriously. To jump a Crip was serious. Even though the Bloods out numbered the Crips in C-74, the Crips were still a force to be reckoned with. I knew I would see him when I went on the visiting floor. One day me and little ABG was smoking a cigarette in the day room and there was this big guy sitting in front of us. The guy asked me if I can save him some of the cigarette little ABG had already given me half of. I said, "Cool." I asked him where he was from and he lived near my father's house in Brooklyn. We kept talking and we came to find out that we knew most of the same people. He was Blood and everyone called him BROOKLYN. When you first look at him you wouldn't think he was that tough. I mean he was big, but not like Shaquille O'Neal big, he was more like Big Fat Joe Big. But, when he started telling the stories about the old neighborhood I knew he wasn't lying. Even if the story sounded a little embellished this wasn't his first time getting arrested, actually it was his 5th.

He told us about the Building. The Building was where you didn't want to be. We were in the Sprungs, which was a dorm outside, but the Building was all cells and it was inside. He told us about all the people he saw get cut in there. In the Sprungs there were a lot of fights but not a lot of cutting. The Building was the total opposite. I liked Brooklyn. He was cool and Little ABG liked him too. I called my girlfriend that afternoon and she told me she was able to hustle up some money to get me bailed out and that I should be out in a few hours. That was music to my ears. I was finally getting out of this hell hole and I didn't plan on ever coming back. The idea of how she got the money never even crossed my mind. I didn't care as long as I was out of this God forsaken place. The officers told me to pack my belongings. Some of the inmates where watching me as I packed. I wasn't sure if they where angry that I was leaving them, because we all know misery loves company, or more upset that it wasn't them leaving. Again, I didn't care. It was about me right now. I was going to miss ABG and Brooklyn. They were my dogs. They held me down and I could never forget it. Before I left I told ABG I would hold the set down when I got home and I would represent ABG to the fullest. Brooklyn was coming out soon so we made plans to hook up when he go out. I didn't pack much. I left most of my stuff to Brook and ABG. They could have it. They would need it more than me.

I waited in the holding pen for 5 hours. They finally let me out. The bus dropped me off in Queens and I was headed right to my girl's crib. She did me right. I loved her so much. If it wasn't for her I'd still be in there. My mother even tried to convince her to leave me in there. She said that all I was going to do was go back. Can you believe that? I hated her for that. I hated her for everything. I got to my girl's house around 2:30 in the morning. She was waiting for me. I knocked on the window and she came outside in black lingerie. She looked better than I remembered. I gave her a big bear hug and kissed her. She was happy to see me. I was happy too. She had the weed already rolled up for me. That's my girl. She knows just what I need. I smoked and we went inside. I was out of Rikers, and now I was back at home where I was supposed to be.

The next day I went outside to the park with my black bandanna around my head. I told ABG I would be repping the set to the fullest when I got out and that's what I was doing. There were a couple of people that I knew and everyone was curious about the bandana. I told them I was down with a set called ABG and you could tell that they looked at me differently. Fear was in their eyes and I liked it. I liked it a lot. At the time, Bloods were slashing people in their faces for initiation and everyone knew that I was a part of them even though I wasn't a Blood.

I didn't have anywhere to stay out there since my grandfather sold the house and my mother moved to Queens. My mother took me to court and told the judge that she didn't want me living with her anymore. I didn't want to live with her anyway, the judge ordered me to go and live with my father but after the hearing I told my Dad that I'll be fine on my own and left with my girlfriend. I was making some good money selling weed and my girlfriend's cousin's girlfriend lived across the street from a gas station that a lot of my customers went to. I saw this as an opportunity to make more money, so I told my girlfriend to ask her if she could let us stay at the house. She said yes and it was on after that. I started selling weed from across the street. All my clients had to do was stand in front of the gas station and that let me know that they wanted something. I could see them from the window so I was chilling. The money was rolling in faster than ever before. My plan was to save some money so my girl and I could get our own place. I was high, I was getting money, my gear was tight and I was having fun, until my girl's cousins girlfriend   had to come and mess things up. When my girl's cousin's boyfriend, saw how much money we were making she wanted us to hit her off with some dough. I know I should've just given her the money; she was smoking weed for free! She was a smoker. She smoked the weed like they were cigarettes and now she wanted the weed and some money? Hell no! I wasn't about to share and that's what I told her. Guess what she told me? She told me if we don't get the hell out of her house she was going to call the cops on us. I didn't need to be running into any cops right about now. So we bounced. We were running up the street with all of our clothes in a stolen shopping cart from the supermarket. She was crazy enough to really call the cops. We didn't know where to go. We were out in the street with no where to go. We decided to see of the key to my old house still worked. My grandfather sold the house but the people didn't move in yet. It was worth a try...so we did... Guess what? The key still worked! We had the house all to ourselves.

I was still hustling weed around town. I managed to get a job working at a factory an hour away from my house. It wasn't really worth it but during the day I needed something to do because no one was outside during the day and that made me all the more noticeable to the cops. I got the job from one of Natasha's uncles. He hooked me up. He was a cool cat that just came home from doing 10 years in the joint. When I would come home I would find Natasha cooking dinner for us. For a minute it felt like we had our own house, I loved her so much. She was my first love. My fantasy soon came to an end one night when my grandfather came to the house to remove some of his remaining furniture and smelled weed as soon as he walked through the door. He was banging on the basement door for us to come out. He had the keys to every door in the house so it was a matter of time before he figured out that he had them. We ran and hid under the stairs. He came downstairs and was pissed. He knew we were there, or at least knew that I was there but thought that we left before he came. We couldn't stay there and her mother sure wasn't letting me sleep at her house.

She caught me spending the night over her house too many times already. I decided that I was going to spend the night at my Dad's house in Brooklyn and just travel to her during the day. Both of us weren't really feeling the idea but we had no other options.

Chapter Fourteen

A New Fling

Brooklyn was just how I left it, dirty. Everything was ghetto and hood. There were some good parts, especially where my father lived. He lived near the Jews and the Pakistanians, right off of Coney Island Avenue. My father was surprised to see me. I told him that I was looking for a job and was saving money so that I could get an apartment for me and Natasha to stay in. He shook his head and said nothing. Just like old times. I rarely saw him at the house. He was either at work or preaching at a revival. That was cool with me. I didn't want him to see me when I was high anyway. I met up with my boy, Brooklyn that I met in jail. He got out a few weeks after I did. All the stories he told me about his crew when we were locked up were all true. We would all get high and they would laugh at the stuff they used to do. I'm not talking about building tree houses or being boy scouts but I'm talking about having gang fights and even fighting cops. They were the real deal. All of them had felonies and all of them were carrying a piece (gun). They made me feel like I knew them for years. They treated me like family. It was the first time I really felt part of something. All of them were Blood and I was the only one repping ABG. We drank and smoked literally . On Fridays we would find parties to go to. One Friday we went to this party on 21st and I met Kema. She was of a light complexion with beautiful skin and light brown eyes. She was slim and it looked like when she turned 18 every man with a mouth would try to holla at her. She looked so good. The DJ played Jamaican music and we danced to that all night. We were grinding so hard on each other we felt like we were in there by ourselves. I asked her for her phone number and she gave it to me.

I was going out to Long Island to see my girlfriend but not as often as I was before I hooked up with Brooklyn and his crew. When I finally saw my girlfriend, she was so mad. I hadn't seen her in 2 weeks. I promised her that I would come see her every day and that made her feel better. I went to see her every day for 2 months. Some days I would just spend the night at her house without her mom knowing. But sometimes her mom would find me and kick me out in the middle of the night. That was the worst. After getting kicked out and not having enough money in my pocket to re-up and buy some more weed to sell, I decided that she would have to come see me at my dad's house and that I would be hanging out more often in Brooklyn.

When I went back around 21st and hooked up with Brooklyn and his boys they all treated me like I never left. I made sure that my gear was tight every time I went out there. I had to. One day Brooklyn, Lee (Brooklyn's best friend) and I were chilling on the steps of a building on 21st. We just finished smoking 2 blunts and we were about to get some Hennessey. While we were sitting down 2 girls started walking towards us. One of the girls was brown skinned with chinky eyes. She had a nice body, but the girl she was walking with almost made me fall off the steps. This was the 'baddest' girl I'd ever seen in my life. I know there are levels of beauty but this girl was at the highest. She was redbone, with dark hair, chinky eyes, no stomach and her body said, "look at me." She had on a pair of tight guess jeans and a halter top that revealed her neck and back. Not one spot was on her body. I couldn't believe she was walking towards us. Brooklyn got up and said, "What's up?" and gave them both a hug. I couldn't believe that he knew both of them, especially redbone and so did Lee. Brooklyn introduced me to them. I licked my dry weed lips and mustered up enough air in my body to say "what's up?" Luckily, my voice didn't crack. I had never seen a girl this bad before. Redbone's name was Sophie and her friends name was China. She went inside the building that we were sitting in. She lived on the 4th floor. After they went upstairs I asked Brooklyn what was up with her. He said that everybody was trying to holla at her but she wasn't giving anyone play.

Forget Kema, forget Natasha. I wanted Sophie. "She was out of my league", I said to myself. That made me want her more. She looked so good. She never saw me around there before and everyone out there knew I was about my paper. I was out there drinking and smoking every day and I was making no money. After seeing her I hustled up some money and got back on my grind. She was my motivation. I had to be fly and have money in my pocket. And I did. Every time I went around the way I made sure I was dressed fresh to death. I matched from head to toe. And everything was new. I never wore the same thing twice and everyone knew that, so did Sophie. I would say "what's up?" every time I saw her but never made my move. The time wasn't right.

One day I went to building 218 and waited for someone to open the main door. I went right to the 4th floor and knocked on the first door that I saw. I didn't know which apartment was hers but I didn't care. There were only

3 choices and if the first one wasn't it, it had to be one of the others. A Caucasian couple lived in there. Behind the second door an Asian couple lived in. She had to be in door number 3. Behind door number 3 was the 'baddest' girl you could imagine. She had on a tank top, short shorts, and I mean short, and those fuzzy slippers with the bunny ears. She looked puzzled when she saw me outside. I said "what's up?" and she said the same in return. I asked her if she could come out into the hall so I could talk to her for a second. She said, "cool". I was looking extra fresh that day and I could tell that she was checking me out. The new Jordans didn't even come out and I had them on my feet already. She came out into the hall and I told her that I was feeling her and wanted to know what's good. She smiled. When she smiled I melted. I was standing in front of one of the 'baddest' girls I had ever seen with my two eyes and she was smiling at me. She told me that she was talking to someone but it was nothing serious. I said the same. I felt a little bad but come on now. No guy would pass up an offer like this one and I mean no guy. We talked in her hallway for 2 hours about different topics.

She was real down to earth and was real cool. She just made me like her more. She gave me her number and told me to call her. I asked her for a hug and she gave it to me. I wanted to hold her for the rest of my life. I looked her in the eyes and went to kiss her. She let me. I kissed her like I was making a movie. It was the best kiss I ever had. Our tongues danced like me and Kema's at the party. I don't remember how long we kissed but when it was over, there was nothing either of us could say but, later. I don't remember how I got home or how long it took me to get there. I know I walked but I don't remember walking. All I could think about was her face, her smile and that kiss.

When I went back out to Long Island to see Natasha, I didn't feel as bad as I thought I would. I didn't act any different around her. But I did think about Sophie constantly. When I wasn't with Natasha, I was with Sophie.

Sophie didn't know I had a girlfriend, she just knew I was getting money. Hustling was my way of dealing with both of them. I had to keep going to Long Island because that's where most of my customers were. And I had to go to Brooklyn because that's where my dad and my connect were. It was the perfect situation. Money was coming in, my gear was tight and Sophie loved me.

One night I invited Sophie and China over to my brother's spot in Queens. It was really my mother's house but my brother had to stay there because that's where he got paroled to. When China saw my brother she was on his top (she was sweating him). My brother was diesel (muscular) and it was noticeable, especially since he didn't like to wear shirts. Him and China was kicking it while me and Sophie were in the corner chatting. We decided to go for a walk around the block and smoke some weed. My brother didn't smoke so I didn't even offer him. He wouldn't accept anyway but he did drink. We stopped at the liquor store and brought a big bottle of E & J. We were done that night. The memory of that night is kind of sketchy but one thing I do remember is that Sophie and I didn't do nothing that night, and I mean nothing. After we smoked 2 blunts and drunk the whole bottle, she was talking about stupid stuff. I mean stupid. Her age really came out that night. I just wanted to go to sleep be cause she was draining me.

Part VI
One more chance...

Chapter Fifteen

The Job

   December 13, 1999: I was so high. I had never been that high before. I mean I smoked every kind of weed on the planet, so I thought. But this had to be the best weed I ever smoked in my life. I couldn't get any higher if I tried, trust me. I had already tried. I tried to smoke as much as I could because I knew I would never be able to smoke weed like that again. This was how I was thinking on my first trip to Jamaica and I planned on it actually being my last. My best friend D got murdered three months earlier and I was low on cash, really low. My girlfriend wanted this expensive chain and bracelet for Christmas and I wasn't about to tell her no. I would do anything for that girl.

   I met D's cousins a few times in the past. They were cool. One was Mitchell and the other was Ken. They were both Jamaican. I reached out to them after D's murder because they knew how tight we were, and I was hoping they would be able to hook me up with some cash or some work (another term for drugs). Everyone knew that these cats had money. D was making $6-7,000 a day and they had to be making more than he was. They were into "big money". The type of money that you only have to make one run a week and you had $100,000 in the trunk of your car. I spoke to Mitch and told him my predicament. After I explained everything to him he told me that he had a job for me that could put me back on my feet for a few months. I was all ears.

He had a girl that went to Jamaica for him every 3 months and came back with cocaine sewn into the bottom of a suitcase. The girl had gotten sick and they needed someone to take her place. The first thing that popped into my mind wasn't the danger of drug trafficking; it wasn't the possibility of getting killed in Jamaica by someone I didn't even know; it wasn't even the fact that you can do 25 years in a maximum security prison. The first thing that I asked him was "How much was I going to get paid for this job?" I was only interested in the money. He told me he would pay me $10,000. Half of which I would receive before I left and the other half I would receive when I came back. That was music to my ears.

The night I was leaving I was so excited. All I could think about was having that $10,000 in my hand and my girlfriend's face when I showed up with her chain and bracelet set in my hand. That night we had sex. It was like we were having sex for the last time. I was only going to Jamaica for 3 days and coming right back. She told me to be careful and that she loved me. Mitch drove me to the airport and told me that if anything didn't look right or feel right, just to leave the suitcase and get back on the plane. I told him ok, but leaving the bag was the last thing on my Mind. He put $5,000 in my hand and told me that I would get the rest when I came back, with the bag of course.

The flight was pretty smooth. The food was decent and I sat by myself. When I arrived in Montego Bay airport, it was like I was on another planet. As soon as I grabbed my bag and went outside I saw a tall man in a uniform with glasses, holding an M-16 in his hand. I was shocked. I never saw an M-16 up close like that before and the man's face said that he wouldn't be afraid to use it. I looked around for the man that was supposed to be picking me up and he was holding a sign with my name on it. The man had to be 6'2 and weighed about 180 lbs, wore black sunglasses and dreadlocks. His name was Reddy. He seemed pretty cool but it was hard for me to make out what he was saying most of the time. His accent was so strong I kept asking him to repeat what he said. He took me to this little house and I mean little literally. It was the neighborhood store I was told and Reddy lived in a small cottage behind it. From the back of the store you could see the entire city. The view was beautiful.

Reddy introduced me to the man that I would actually be staying with and his name was Damien. Damien had to be in his late 40's, 5'8 and weighed somewhere around 170 lbs. He dressed very conservatively and sounded educated when he spoke. Damien asked me if I wanted something to eat. I said, "yes" and he asked me to pick from McDonalds or KFC. I told him neither, I was actually hoping to eat some Jamaican food. They laughed and gave me five. I asked them if they had any weed and they laughed even harder. Reddy pulled out a Ziploc bag full of weed. My eyes lit up. When I rolled up the weed it wasn't like the weed back in New York. I had to actually pull it apart just to get it to fit into the paper I used to roll the weed up in. When I took in the first puff, the smoke hit me like a ton of bricks. I coughed for 5 minutes straight. After I stopped coughing I looked at the weed in my hand and thought to myself, this is the best weed I ever smoked in my life. And I'm going to smoke until I can't smoke any more. I sat in the back of the store overlooking the entire city and smoked 3 joints back to back and I was so high that I couldn't even keep my eyes open. Whenever I closed my eyes I would feel like the world was spinning. After the last joint I went inside the store, sat on the stool and ate the food that they brought me. They brought me fried chicken, rice and peas with plantains. I'm not sure if it was the munchies that I had after I smoked, but that food was slammin! When Reddy and Damien saw how high I was they were laughing. They couldn't believe I smoked that many joints by myself. And I couldn't believe how high I was. I honestly couldn't get any higher. I was sitting on a stool, high as ever, on an island where I just met these two guys with $5,000 in my left pocket and a zip lock bag of weed in my right pocket. And I was having the time of my life.

I woke up to Damien tapping me telling me we had to go. When I asked where we were going he told me to his house because that's where I was sleeping. It was about a twenty minute ride to his house from where we were at. All the roads were dirt roads and everyone drove on the right side instead of the left. When I saw his house I was surprised. It was quite different from Reddy's little shack. He had a 3 bedroom home and he told me that he built it himself. There were some parts of the house that weren't finished yet he said. It took him about 2 years to build that house.

When I walked in his family was at the kitchen table eating supper. He had a five year old son and a wife of 12 years. I said hello to them and followed him into the room I would be sleeping in. I wondered if they knew why I was there. The room was nice, the bed was made and it was clean. When I sat on the bed Damien told me he would be right back, and closed the door behind him. He came in a few seconds later with a suitcase. He told me that this was the briefcase I would use when I went back to New York. I asked him where the coke would be in the suitcase, because I couldn't see where it could possibly be stored without being noticed. He reached towards the bottom of the suitcase and lifted up the bottom part of the suitcase to reveal a false bottom. I was impressed. This was definitely going to work I thought. I told him it sounded good and he left the room again to put the suitcase in another room. When he came back he asked what I wanted to do for the remainder of the evening. I told him I wanted to smoke the rest of the weed in my pocket and go and see some girls. He smiled at me and said "Alright cool mon".

Damien called Reddy to come and pick me up. He said he knew the right spot to take me to. Reddy pulled up in front of the house and we were on our way. When we pulled into the parking lot I wasn't sure if he was taking me to a club or to someone's house. I saw a girl pulling a guy into the alley but I thought they were a couple getting a little freaky. As soon as we got to the front door a girl walked out wearing a thong and some shoes. My eyes popped out of my head. "Hey Daddy!" she said as she walked up the steps. My eyes were glued to her behind as she walked up the steps. Reddy just laughed and said you haven't seen anything yet.

Inside the strip club was like a dream. There were all types of girls of different shapes and sizes. They all had nice bodies and they all had on the same uniform - thongs and shoes. I was apprehensive with them when I first got there. I would watch them dance but as soon as they would look at me I would quickly turn my head. I wasn't a shy person, but watching a girl dance in front of me naked and her knowing that I'm doing so, kind of made me feel a little weird at first. I think Reddy noticed I was a little shy so he asked one of the girls to come and give me a lap dance. She was one of the finest girls I had ever seen, and I mean fine. She was 5'2 brown skinned and had more curves than the letter S. Her grinding and winding had me in a daze. And what was crazy about it is that she liked it. She asked me if I wanted to go to a hotel and I said, "sure".

94

Before I left I was looking for Reddy but I couldn't find him. I'd see him when I come back, I thought. We hopped into a cab and went towards the hotel. Before I even got into the cab I had three problems: The first was I only had a few dollars left on me because I left the rest of the money in Damien's house so I wouldn't spend it and I had the serious munchies because I had smoked some more weed in Reddy's car before we got to the strip club. The second real problem was that I had a girlfriend at home that I didn't want to cheat on (but I was in Jamaica, who would know). And the third was what actually made me tell the cab driver "let's go back", I didn't have any condoms and I never liked using them. My girlfriend and I tried using them two or three times and after that we never used them again. I told the stripper that I didn't have any money and that I only had enough to pay for the cab. When she asked how much I had I showed her what was in my pocket which was only like 20 American dollars. So, we went back to the club and I saw Reddy outside. Reddy asked me what happened and I told him that I didn't have any money to pay her. He called the girl over to him and said something to her in her ear. She looked over at me and shook her head and walked inside. I asked Reddy what just happened and he said he told her that I was from America, and that I really liked her and wanted to sleep with her because she was the only Jamaican girl that I'd ever been with. He asked her if I could have sex with her for 20 American dollars, and she said, "yes". The girl was waiting for me in the bathroom and we could do it in there.

I looked at Reddy and said "good let's go", and I started walking towards the car. He asked me where I was going, and I said to get some more of that good Jamaican food that you brought me earlier. He asked "what about the girl?" I told him if I had to choose between the girl and some food, I would have to choose the food because I had the serious munchies. He chuckled and we left. The truth of the matter was I wasn't trying to sleep with that girl without a condom and get a disease. She was fine but she wasn't that fine.

The next day went by pretty quickly. Damien spent most of the time talking to me about not being nervous and paying attention to small details at the airport. He told me that no one has ever gotten caught and if I stick to the script I would be just fine. Later on in the evening Reddy came over with the suitcase and we all went into the room I was staying in to check it out. Reddy told me that the drugs were in the false bottom of the suitcase and it looked pretty unnoticeable until I touched it. The bottom of the suitcase felt lumpy. It felt like there were a whole bunch of rocks underneath the bottom. I told them I thought it was too lumpy but they assured me it wasn't. In my mind I knew it was lumpy but all I could think about was the other $5,000 I would get in my hand upon my return. The plan was set.

That morning on my way to the airport a lot of thoughts were swimming through my head. I kept thinking about how lumpy the bottom of the suitcase was. It really bothered me. I could hear Mitch's voice telling me to leave the bag if I didn't feel it was right. But all I could think about was the money and what I had already planned on doing with it. The $5,000 that he gave me would be gone in a day. I needed that money and I wasn't leaving that suitcase. The suitcase was my ticket to a better life or so I thought. When I initially got out the car I was tempted to leave the suitcase and run inside the airport. But I didn't. I took it with me. My flight was boarding and I handed my passport over to the lady behind the desk. I was so nervous I could hear my heart beat as they put the suitcase onto the baggage check. It went through the X-ray and they told me where to catch my flight. I was clear. I smiled from ear to ear. I was on the 6:15 pm flight to JFK airport and my money would be waiting for me there once I arrived.

I couldn't really sleep so I just sat there and looked out the window wondering what just happened in the last 72 hours. The flight landed and I was on my way. I got my suitcase from off the carrier and walked towards the baggage check. The man had asked to see my passport and I gave it to him. He entered my name into the computer and looked at it like there was a mistake. I asked him if everything was okay. He looked back at me and asked me if I knew that I had a warrant out for my arrest. A warrant! "No," I replied, and then I remembered. The day I was supposed to go to court was the day I left for Jamaica. My mother had taken me to family court because she wanted to give up custody of me. Shoot! How could I forget that?

I told the officer what the court case was for and it made him look through the suitcase even harder. When he started to take everything out I almost peed in my pants. They didn't take everything out in Jamaica; they just put it through the X-Ray. Every time he took something out my heart got closer and closer to the floor. I wanted to run, but my legs wouldn't move. I saw the officer reach for the bottom of the suitcase and begin feeling the bottom of it. He pulled a little knife from out of his back pocket and he poked the bottom of the suitcase with it. He took the blade out of the suitcase, turned to the other officer that was searching someone else's luggage and whispered in his ear "I found his drugs". In that split second the only thing I could think about was Psalms 23, the Lord is my Shepherd. Until this very day I still don't know why that was the first thing to pop into my head but it didn't matter. The cold of the silver bracelets snapped me out of my daze. I went quietly with the officers as they escorted me to the back room.

When I got into the back room I could hear the other officers telling the guy that found the drugs, 'good job'. I didn't know what to do, think or say when I sat on that bench. The only thing I could do was close my eyes and wish I was somewhere else. I could hear my mother's voice loud and clear "If you bail him out, he's just going to get arrested again." Boy was she right. I put my legs up on the bench, faced the wall and went to sleep. They say you can tell if a man is guilty of a crime, all you have to do is watch how he acts when he's in the jail cell. He would be the one sleeping. And I slept for what seemed to be hours. The odd thing was that the sleep was the best sleep I had in a long time.

I awoke to have an officer read me my rights and then shove me into a smaller room with a mirror on the wall. He told me to have a seat. He asked if I wanted anything to drink and I told him "no". I didn't know what was going to happen but I knew that I definitely wasn't going home tonight. He asked a whole bunch of questions about what was I doing with the drugs? Who was I bringing it to? and a whole bunch of other questions. I told them that I had no idea how the drugs got into my bag. They could tell I was lying but I stuck to the same story.

After the three hour interrogation the detectives allowed me to make one phone call. I knew who I had to call but I know who I didn't want to call. I could hear her voice now "I told you not to bail him out; he's not gonna do nothing but get locked up again". I dialed my mother's home number and my brother answered. When I told my brother that I got arrested again he was upset. When I told him what I was arrested for, he had no words. There was silence on the phone for about 2 minutes. My mother was in the background asking what happened. He told her that I got locked up again and she was silent too. We stayed on the phone for 15 minutes but for more than half of the phone call we were silent. I could hear my mother crying in the background. I told myself I shouldn't have called. I told my brother I would call when I got to Rikers because I knew I wasn't coming home for a very long time. He said ok and we hung up.

I let my family down and I felt bad for doing it. My brother had just come home from doing 18 months in jail. I was arrested 30 days after I was released for gun possession. My girlfriend bailed me out and here I go, less than two months later, I get arrested again. "It's time to go" the officers said, and with that I was on a one way bus going to Riker's Island. I don't know what I dreaded most. The fact that I might be doing 25 years like the detective told me, or the fact that I'm going back to Riker's Island. I barely made it out of there the first time and now I was going back for a longer time.

I was on Rikers Island for one year. I was placed in a house with other inmates that had high profile cases. I was sentenced to 4-12 years. They ran both charges (gun and drug) concurrently. I wouldn't be able to go to any special drug programs because of the gun charge, it was classified as a violent crime and all drug programs required that inmates not have any violent felonies. I really didn't know how much drugs was in the suitcase but it was enough to keep me out of the federal prison system. Of all the things that had done, this by far was the dumbest. But if I wasn't in jail, I probably would have been on the street dead. Rikers is what I called a living hell. It was here I saw the most fights, the most stabbings and the most deaths. My house, (C-74) 1 Upper North Southside, not to be confused with Southside where all the homosexuals were placed, was a house filled with inmates that had the most heinous crimes. Let's start with the Mexican. He was locked up for cutting his boss up with a butcher knife because he refused to pay him for the hours that he had worked. Then we had Ty and Charles. They were locked up for the cab driver killings in East New York. They both were 17 and they were facing life in prison. They told me when they went to court people were outside protesting that life was not enough and they should get the death penalty. We had the church boy. Church boy was locked up for killing the Chinese delivery

man in Queens with a brick. He was 16. We had the kid
that shot someone over a quarter in Brooklyn. We had
Blanco, who shot and robbed the parents of a famous New
York City detective. The list went on. Every day we fought.
Every day we jumped someone and some days I didn't even
want to be a part of what was going on. But I had no
choice. I either jumped in with them or they jumped me. It
didn't matter who you were. The same rules applied for
everyone. Almost everyone was in a gang. Everyone
was either a Crip or a Latin King. The Mexicans were a part
of MS13 and everyone knew they didn't play. The only
person that was Blood was my boy, Brooklyn. He came back
to Rikers for shooting up some Crips on Caton Avenue in
Brooklyn and this time he was facing some serious charges.
His story was on the news, so they sent him to my house. I
had to have a meeting with all of the leaders of the house
just to ensure that no one touched him. I told them that he
was my cousin, and because I was in the house the longest,
they granted him immunity.

After being on Rikers for a year, I was then sent up
North. Now if I thought Rikers was hell, up North has no
words to describe it. I was sent to Washington Correctional
Facility. I saw some people that I was on Rikers with and
some showed me love and some didn't. Every other day
someone was getting slashed in the face, so I had to make
sure I was hanging around the right people. I kept a razor
on me and every second just in case I needed to protect
myself. Waking up every day not knowing if you were going
to be sleeping in your bed at the dorm or the bed in the
infirmary will eventually change you. I had one fight on
Rikers that I won, but even after I won the fight I almost
died. The person I fought was Blood and all his fellow Bloods
wanted to jump me but I was sent up North the next day. It
was in prison I read my first book. It was called "Makes me
wanna holla" by Nathan McCall. That book really had an
effect on me. After reading that book, I read every book that
I put my hands on. The next book I read was "Malcolm x" by

Alex Haley. That book changed my life. It was up North that I really started to think about all of the things I had been through. My family and my grandmother they all came to mind there. I missed my grandmother. I remembered all of the words that she said to me. How I should stay away from trouble and not let the things my parents put us through affect us. But how could we not. Up North all I did was work out and read. I read books on world religions, western philosophy, Christianity, you name it, and I read it. I even earned my GED in prison. Getting my GED meant a lot to me. It made me feel like I wasn't stupid. It made me feel that I could actually go to college. It gave me the confidence to know that I could actually have a future. None of my friends had gone or were going to college. Everyone I knew was hustling. No one wrote me except my mother and my brother. Natasha wrote me for a while and even came to see me a few times. The letters eventually stopped coming and so did the visits. I did one year up North. One day as I was reading J.A. Rogers, "Superman to man" and the officer on duty told me to start packing my things. "Where am I going?" I asked. He told me that I was being sent to a drug program in Staten Island which meant I would be closer to home. I asked how I had gotten into the program. He told me that my violent felony was overturned into a non-violent felony. I don't know how it happened because I never put in for it, I thought to myself. It didn't matter to me, as long as I was going home early. I was happy. My mother was coming to see me every weekend so when I called her and told her she was happy. When my mother would come see me we would have heart to heart talks. I told her that I loved her and that she really hurt me by moving so much. She told me that she was sorry and that she had changed her life around. Before then, we never had conversations like that. She was going to this church faithfully and she even bought me a cassette tape of their choir. I listened to it and I liked it. The name of the church was Love Fellowship Tabernacle, and the Pastor was Hezekiah Walker. I had never heard of him before but my mother mentioned that he was supposed to be a famous singer.

I was transported to Arthur Kill Correctional Facility in Staten Island and it was there I spent my last year of my prison sentence. Arthur Kill was a decent prison although our housing officer was a jerk, but besides him it was cool. I had no fights. It was just people there serving their time. Nobody wanted to fight because they would just ship you upstate and you would be further away from your family. If I wasn't reading I was working out. Day in and day out I would read. Once I read 4 books in 5 days. I never did that before. It was now that I understood why my cousin Marcy would always have a book in her hand when we weren't allowed to watch TV as kids.

Towards the end of my sentence my father came to see me. It was awkward. I was happy he came and I had so much to say, but I didn't say it. We spoke about what was going on now, but we didn't speak about the things that had happened in the past. I was happy to see him. I wondered if he felt that any of this was his fault. Even my brother came to see me. He couldn't come see me before because he was still on parole. I was happy to see him. He had joined the church that my mother was going to and he said that when I came out he wanted me to come and visit, I told him I would. My cousins came to see me, Marcy, Venice and Susan. That was a hard visit. It was almost like they wanted to say, your mother should have left you with us. When I looked at their faces it reminded me of the night we left. We all had tears in our eyes, and this time we had the same tears but for different reasons. Their older cousin who was always loud and funny was now also in prison. We didn't dwell on that too long. We all knew I was coming out in a few months so we were talking about what we were going to do when I got out. Natasha never came to see me but surprisingly Sophie did. I was glad when I saw her, she looked good. I mean real good. I really liked Sophie.

One night before it was time for me to leave I had a dream. In the dream I saw my grandmother standing next to an angel. I called out to my grandmother and she just waved to me and walked away. I kept calling her and she just walked away. I didn't understand the dream but I knew something was funny when my grandmother wasn't at the visit. I later found out that my grandmother died from a stroke while I was on Rikers. No one told me because they were afraid of how I would react to the news. My only regret was that I didn't get to say goodbye.

Chapter Sixteen

I'm Home

I was happy to be home. Well, half way home that is. I was put on work release, which meant I had to work to stay out of prison. It was granted to people who they felt were reformed while in prison. As soon as I came home my family threw me a party at my mother's house. All of my cousins were there and Mono, and Gladys. I was happy to see everyone. My father actually picked me up and drove me there. He was happy to see me and I was happy to see him. He was surprised to see how big I had gotten from working out. My brother was still working out while I was in prison so when I came home we looked like 2 huge buildings!

My mother was the happiest I had ever seen her. She couldn't stop hugging me. She came to see me for 3 years straight. Everything she had ever done to me was null and void. She made up for it. This was the first time I could say that I truly loved my mother and that I had no hate in my heart for her. She wasn't the greatest mother in the beginning but she was a wonderful mother in the end.

My mother and brother took me to church with them, I promised them I would go. To be honest I really wasn't focused on church. But when I went, the church was packed like how my grandfather's church used to be before it split. I went there in jeans and a t-shirt only to find that everyone was wearing the same thing. I never saw that before. My brother introduced me to a lot of people but only 2 of them stood out to me. One of them was this cat named Kevin. You could tell he worked out and there was something about him that reminded me about my boy D. I liked him as soon as I met him (pause). He was a real dude you could tell from the jump (immediately). And the other one was this girl named Margie. She looked a lot like Sophie, but better. She was Spanish and she had light brown eyes. She looked good. I mean real good. Most of the other people he introduced me too, I forgot their names. We got a seat and I listened to Pastor Hezekiah Walker talk about my whole life. Everything he said was like he was talking directly to me. The more he talked the more I wanted to just crawl under one of the chairs. Everything he was saying applied to everything I was going through. He spoke about forgiveness and how the things that you go through make you stronger. As he preached people would get up and say "amen", or "preach". I just sat there with tears in my eyes thinking about D, my grandmother and my father. I looked over and saw my mother saying "amen" and remembered the nights that she came into the house drunk, and now she was sober and in church. I looked at my brother and remembered all the times he was high and drunk and now he was sitting in church sober and changed. I wanted to be changed. I wanted to start all of over. I wanted a new life. The pastor asked if anyone wanted to accept Jesus Christ as their Lord and savior and before he could even finish his sentence I was already walking down the aisle towards him. The words he preached pricked my heart and I wanted a change in my life. As I walked down the aisle my brother walked with me. Tears were in my eyes as I thought about the last 5 years of my life. I was tired. I wanted a new beginning. People were clapping as I walked down there. They made me feel good. As I got to the front of the church there were other people that wanted to change their lives also. The preacher looked at me and said, "We've been praying for you son." No words could express how I felt at that moment. I broke down and started to weep like a little baby. Until then I hadn't cried in 3 years and I was well over due. I began to think about how I was living my life. The drugs, the weed, the guns, the gangs, the sex, the parties...everything. I did all those things because I was trying to fit in, and be a part of something. To be loved by someone. Accepted by people. I wanted to be part of a family. I was looking for a father in boys and seeking for a mother in girls. Looking for peace in weed and seeking joy in parties. I was running from pain towards destruction. I was looking for love in all the wrong places. Inside I was empty. I was always existing but   never living. Three years of my life were taken away from me. But in all actuality, I was in Prison before I even went to jail. I was confined in the prison cell of Abandonment, and shackled next to Low Self Esteem. I went to the mess hall with Resentment and went to bed with Loss of Identity. I wanted to start over. I needed a second chance at life. Pastor Walker told me that Jesus came that I might have life, and have it more abundantly. I grew up in church and this was the first time I ever listened to what the preacher was saying. I realized though my father wasn't there as much as he should have been, there was someone watching over me the whole time. My real Father. He spoke to me just as much my dad did, but He did more for me than my father could ever do. At that very moment, I was changed. I accepted Jesus Christ as my Lord and Savior and ever since that day I have never been the same. Jesus changed my life. That chapter in my life is over and thus begins my new chapter. The pastor prayed for me and I walked out of that church a new man. "Behold, old things are pass away..." I now had a reason to live. I was determined to make this life better than my last one. No more drugs, no more liquor, no more hustling and no more gangs. I wanted to be like my mother and my brother. Changed.

To be continued.

Check out the Official Jeffrey Barlatier Page
At:
www.myspace.com/jeffreybarlatier

Post a comment, tell a friend, and order a copy for a loved one.

Look out for the sequel to Street Dreams for God's Child. Entitled:

Street Dreams for God's Child, After the Altar.

Jeffrey Barlatier

.

Jeffrey Barlatier